ANT & DEC

ANT & DEC

Loving every second !

BY ALEC LOM

CENTURY

Published by Century in 2002

1 3 5 7 9 10 8 6 4 2

First published in the United Kingdom in 2002 by Century

The Random House Group Limited
20 Vauxhall Bridge Road, London SW1V 2SA

Random House Australia (Pty) Limited
20 Alfred Street, Milsons Point, Sydney,
New South Wales 2061, Australia

Random House New Zealand Limited
18 Poland Road, Glenfield
Auckland 10, New Zealand

Random House South Africa (Pty) Limited
Endulini, 5a Jubilee Road, Parktown 2193, South Africa

The Random House Group Limited Reg. No. 954009

www.randomhouse.co.uk

A CIP catalogue record for this book is available from the British Library
Papers used by Random House are natural, recyclable products made from wood grown in sustainable forests. The manufacturing processes conform to the environmental regulations of the country of origin

ISBN 0 7126 22748

Typeset by Andrea Purdie

Printed and bound in Germany by
Appl, Wemding

For Herbert and Dina

Acknowledgments

Contrary to the suggestion on the front cover that I alone am responsible for creating this book, my labours would not have been possible without the help and guidance of many people. I would especially like to thank Hannah Black, Mark Booth and the whole team at Century, with whom it is a genuine pleasure to work; the ever-supportive Jonathan Lloyd and Tara Wynne at Curtis Brown; and the resourceful Rita Gormley, who has done a simply 'bee-yoo-diful' job picture researching. For their speedy assistance, I am indebted to the lovely Annie, and to Phil, both of whom I hope to see a lot more of real soon! Thanks, too, to Geordie superstars Charlie Miller, Carol Ho-Yen and Lynn Chambers for their local knowledge and patient dialect coaching. Big respect to Peter Greenhalgh, who pulled out all the stops and also saved my bacon when my computer crashed. Basil Rider and Nick know how much I appreciated their precious time. Canny Tom Patterson and friends at the *Newcastle Journal*, a great newspaper, deserve a special mention for their kind co-operation. I remain ever grateful to the hard-working, loyal trio, Susan Dunkley, Sally Barney and Alison Ward. Apologies to Sian James - this book is why I missed your Christmas party! Finally, for keeping a secret for so long, thanks to four of Ant and Dec's most devoted fans, thirtysomethings Anne-Marie and Richard Parker, also Barney, 10, and Rosie, six. That leaves my biggest acknowledgment till last – that being married to a writer is hell, a daily frustration, a constant irritation, an utter aggravation. Thank you, dear Sara, for covering for me just occasionally over the past couple of days …

Contents

Author's Note

In 2001 the nation caught the Ant and Dec bug – there is no known antidote. Young and old, North and South, all across the land, millions of us were smitten. Britain's most famous Geordies were rarely off our screens, hosting the Brit Awards, fronting not one or two but a string of their own TV shows like *Slap Bang*, *SM:tv Live*, *Pop Idol* and *Record of the Year*. There can't have been many presenters who enjoyed more air time than the two canny young pretenders down from Newcastle. When they occasionally strayed from the studio, it was only to pop across town to some posh hotel or other, or to London's Royal Albert Hall, to pick up various gongs and trophies, like the one handed them at the National TV Awards, where viewers voted them Britain's Most Popular Entertainers.

Readers' polls in several magazines voted the happy-go-lucky boys 'Stars of the Year'. And behind the scenes, rival television executives, acknowledging their soaring profile, continued to battle and scheme, trying to lure the two presenters with big money contracts and promises of special treatment. No wonder Ant and Dec never stopped smiling and laughing! They did the latter, by the way, all the way to the bank, thanks to a humungous ITV pay cheque.

In another newspaper poll just before Christmas, Ant and Dec were officially voted 'Britain's Best Mates'. The survey asked people aged between 18 and 45 what they thought friendship meant in the 21st century and who was the best example of comradeship today. The popular Tyneside pair's on-screen chemistry earned them the title, beating Dawn French and Jennifer Saunders, and DJs Sara Cox and Zoe Ball.

Inexplicably, however, I have discovered while researching this book that, despite their great success, not all Ant and Dec fans are prepared to stand up and be counted. Most will openly admit to being addicted to their programmes but a minority prefers to remain firmly 'in the closet', claiming instead that the television just happens to be on at the time, or that, of course, it's the children who are the real fans.

So without more ado, I feel I ought to come 'out of the closet' myself. After all, millions of 'Trekkies' do it. Yes, I am prepared to be named and shamed. I am a mad 'Ant'n'Deckie'. And proud of it.

My six-year-old gets in a terrible frenzy every Saturday morning, trying to guess the identity of this week's Wonkey Donkey character. (And no [sigh] she never gets it to rhyme.) Then there's my 10-year-old, who roars with laughter every time Dec sets the scene for the Killer Question in Challenge Ant with the exact same words each week: 'You join us at a very tense moment in the studio ...'

When the brainy contestant beats Ant, my son leaps off the sofa to join in the chant: 'You're thick, you're thick, you're thick, you're thick, thick, thick, thick ...'

Then there are the legions of teenage girl fans, so besotted with their heart-throb idols that they'd do *anything*, go *anywhere*, to meet them, hug them, snog them, marry them, have their babies.

Just take a surfing trip on the internet, type in 'Ant and Dec', click on 'fans' and you'll meet them. They're out there, in their millions. At Ant and Dec's concerts and public appearances, these are the ear-splitting, frenzied girls who hurl knickers and bras up on stage. Some of you who remember Tom Jones in his youth might think that all this is nothing new. But you'd be wrong. Tom never had to suffer what Ant and Dec have. The Voice from the Valleys never had tubes of Smarties and teddy bears thrown at his head.

Our two lovable Geordie urchins are also regarded as compulsive viewing by undergraduates, college students and twentysomethings, who would wake up every Saturday morning, peer groggily out from under the duvet and tune in just in time to catch the opening bars of the *SM:tv Live* signature tune. Ant and Dec quit the series in December 2001, leaving co-host Cat Deeley in charge, but their memory lives on.

Parents in their 30s are equally big fans, nonchalantly loitering by the telly and sinking down to join their kids on the couch. The sound of Cat wishing viewers good morning is often accompanied by the plink-plink-fizz of a couple of Alka-Seltzers after the heavy night before ... which is how Ant and Dec have acquired the tag 'Hangover TV'.

One dad, a viewer in his 40s, sent Ant and Dec a photo of himself the other week. He was pictured holding his index finger about a foot above his face. Attached to the end of his digit, and leading straight down into his right nostril, was, he claimed, Britain's longest bogey. In an accompanying letter, the man explained that he carefully stored the giant piece of snot in the family freezer at home – and his wife kept threatening to defrost it …

Anyway, whoever you are, whatever generation you belong to, this book is for you. Ant and Dec have recently been described as Britain's best new double act since Morecambe and Wise. In their heyday, Eric and Ernie and their famous theme tune *Bring Me Sunshine* brought pleasure to millions. Here's hoping that, with their own special brand of cheeky charm and humour, the Tyneside Twosome McPartlin and Donnelly continue to bring sunshine into our lives for many years to come.

Alec Lom
May 2002

From Newcastle with Love

Have you noticed? Over the past few years, Britain has developed an enormous affection for all things Geordie. With their famous, characteristic Tyneside twang, Geordie actors bring their own special brand of charisma to television series like *The Likely Lads*, *When the Boat Comes In*, *Auf Wiedersehen Pet*, *Byker Grove*, and *Spender*. Geordies who play romantic leads on screen, like the boyishly handsome Robson Green, who first found fame as fusilier David Tucker in ITV's *Soldier, Soldier*, are idolised by millions and snapped up by television executives shelling out multi-million-pound 'golden handcuff' deals. Geordie sportsmen like tearful ex-England international Paul 'Gazza' Gascoigne and Newcastle United's prolific goal-scoring captain Alan Shearer instantly become our heroes. And rock singers with Northeast roots, like Sting (who can make love for hours without tiring) and Jimmy Nail (who can stare blankly for hours without smiling), turn the opposite sex to jelly with their rugged good looks and husky voices.

When it comes to hosting television programmes, there are only two Geordies worth mentioning. Already labelled the 'Morecambe and Wise for the new millennium', the Tyneside Twosome are in their mid-20s but already, as one tabloid headline screamed the other day, 'ANT AND DEC RULE TV!'

Well, why? And how come? They're only 26, after all. Why do we love them so much? And why have they become 'a kind of English institution', as pop star Robbie Williams described them recently?

'a kind of English institution'

When they go home to Newcastle, they are mobbed, just like the Beatles were in Liverpool. Ant and Dec were described at an awards show as 'giants of TV', which made both the boys laugh because they're still knee-high to a grasshopper. [Actually Ant's 5ft 8ins and Dec's 5ft 6ins – Ed.]

So one of the questions addressed in this book is – what is the secret of their success? It can't all simply be down to our enjoyment of their obvious friendship and the instinctive, seemingly unscripted banter that flows freely between them. It is quite remarkable that these two ordinary-looking, unassuming young lads from Newcastle's working-class council estates have risen to become stars with millionaire bank balances and two of the most sought-after faces on British television. No-one in their families can lay claim to a showbusiness background, so it's not as if either of them has followed in the famous footsteps of one of his parents, aunts or uncles.

Crucially though, and more to the point, not only have Ant and Dec risen to the top, they have also proved themselves smart enough to know what constitutes staying power in the world of entertainment. In their 13 years together, as friends and on-screen partners, Anthony McPartlin and Declan Donnelly have come a very long way. Theirs has been, to use the well-worn phrase, a white-knuckle roller-coaster ride. Only those with grit and determination, and a real sense of commitment and dedication, make it to the top like they have.

As they have progressed from teen soap to pop stardom, from TV hosts to mainstream household names, they appear to have moved seamlessly around the business. Like other long-term survivors, for example Sir Cliff or Madonna, they have already proved that they are masters of reinvention.

Of course, their careers as entertainers are still in their infancy. And according to senior industry players, Ant and Dec have a bright future. 'They are very talented as comedians and actors, and their comic timing is very good,' enthuses Lucinda Whiteley, the commissioning editor responsible for taking the pair to Channel 4.

And another expert, this time a highly experienced senior journalist on a leading pop magazine which regularly chooses Ant and Dec as its front-cover pin-ups, reckons, 'I think they'll go on for years. I can see them doing the Royal Variety Performance in 10 years' time. I think their popularity lies in the fact that what you see is what you get. They're very real.'

Long gone are the days when two fresh-faced, wide-eyed and angelic youngsters made their names as naughty teenage schoolboys in the Geordie kids' show *Byker Grove* in the late 1980s and early 90s. But that doesn't mean they have lost any of their boy-next-door charm. They're still the kind of chappies your mum would love to have round for tea – even if their humour is sometimes a little bit close to the bone.

Today, Ant and Dec between them have collected enough trophies to fill several display cabinets. They've won BAFTAs, Royal Television Society Awards, a Bronze Rose of Montreux and several other awards for their TV work. Then there's the Smash Hits Awards and the Brit Award for Best Newcomers. Most pop stars and TV presenters who've been in the business for twice as long cannot rival the silverware these two have collected in the past decade.

But, as the press is quick to point out, too much success too young has turned the heads of many a young star. And Ant and Dec certainly made quite a name for themselves early on in their careers.

But their debut as presenters of their own TV show, *The Ant and Dec Show* at the BBC, was not without its critics and, after changes were made to the programme, audiences dwindled and the duo made the switch to Channel 4. Despite the defection, the show did not do as well as expected. And some pundits believe that these early setbacks may have contributed toward the twosome's humility today.

Experienced agents and producers within the industry will always tell you that when presenters believe they are invulnerable, simply untouchable, the best in the biz and invincible in the ratings, that's when they can, and very often do take a fall. Ant and Dec, perhaps through some early failures, have managed to avoid the arrogance that sometimes accompanies youthful celebrity.

They know only too well who got them their Telstar record deal – it was their *Byker Grove* fans who bombarded the company and the BBC with requests for PJ and Duncan's record. Ant and Dec are humble enough to acknowledge this publicly, frequently choosing newspaper interviews to express their debt of gratitude to their loyal fans.

And talking of the press, Ant and Dec both undoubtedly owe a great deal to their two local newspapers, the *Newcastle Journal* and the *Newcastle Evening Chronicle*. Both papers have followed the lads' careers from their early days on *Byker Grove* to the present day, devoting thousands of column inches to the boys who became two of Tyneside's favourite sons.

One veteran senior journalist on the *Journal* who has monitored their progress since the 1980s sounded modest when I suggested the two presenters owe much to the support their local press has shown them over the years. But it's true, and Ant and Dec would acknowledge that. They both believe in putting back what they can into the region, through their support of local charities and by making personal appearances at corporate events that help to boost the Northeast's economy. The press, particularly in the shape of the *Journal* and the *Chronicle*, are always there to record the event and report the news to Ant and Dec's army of Geordie fans.

And it's the fans, both on Tyneside and across the country, who are so important to Ant and Dec. The boys know full well that ITV doesn't throw multi-million-pound exclusive contracts their way just because they're handsome lads or because someone in authority likes the cut of their jib. It's because the twosome have become a surefire bet to deliver the ratings. They're now known as a safe pair of hands in the business; they're young and upwardly mobile with a great future ahead of them.

They left the BBC's *Live and Kicking* dead and buried, killing off the rival kids' show once and for all. Officially, they weren't supposed to display too much joy and glee at the opposition's demise. That might have been construed as unprofessional in some quarters. But privately, Ant and Dec will tell you that they regarded this as a huge triumph, a victory that absolutely delighted and thrilled them both. And the reason why *SM:tv Live* and *cd:uk* soared in the ratings and gave the BBC such a drubbing is that Ant and Dec never talk down to their audience – unlike too many of the BBC's children's presenters.

'*We treat the viewers — of all ages — with the respect they deserve,*' *say the Geordie comedy duo.*

As a pair, their friendship and closeness are well documented. They work together and socialise together. When they party, they admit to enjoying a drink or three but they stay out of trouble. They don't fall flat on their faces as they leave the film premiere, and they don't trash nightclubs or punch paparazzi photographers outside Groucho's. At home in London, Ant and Dec live two doors away from each other in the same cul-de-sac, and they go on holiday together with their girlfriends. It's almost like a marriage, they admit. Pretty scary. But their friendship rubs off on us. They appear unpretentious, normal – the sort of guys you'd be happy to take down the pub with you (in contrast to some other presenters who are definitely 'peas above sticks' and appear to be graduates of the Hyacinth Bucket Finishing School).

It was their former manager, Dave Holly in Newcastle, who was the first to put his finger on one of the reasons why the duo are a success – it's their partnership itself. As Dave puts it, 'It's one thing getting one person who is good. Here you've got two people who can work together. If you asked me, "What is it that Ant and Dec have that nobody else has?" I wouldn't know. They don't do anything particularly well: they're not the best singers, the best dancers, the best comedians. The best thing about Ant and Dec is … Ant and Dec.'

Their *Byker Grove* producer Matthew Robinson offered Ant and Dec some crucial early advice, possibly the best advice they've ever had. He recalls telling them, 'I suggest you two never fall out, and stick together for as long as you can – as actors, singers or comedians. That is the one piece of advice I give to you.' And it seems to have paid off.

Another thing that makes the lads inseparable is their love of football. Whether you're a soccer fan or not, you can't help but admire two undeniably wealthy and successful television presenters who tell you that they'd willingly give it all up tomorrow for a chance to represent their home town or their country on the football field.

Ant, who dreamt of being a professional footballer at school, discovered early on in his friendship with Dec that they were both passionate Newcastle United fans. For them, nothing in the world can compare with the thrill of watching their beloved Magpies in action on a Saturday afternoon. Both of them miss their home city when they're working down in London and they have insisted repeatedly that they'd happily swap everything they have achieved in showbusiness for a black and white striped shirt and a place in the dressing room at St James' Park.

After *SM:tv Live* made them household names, ITV is reported to have offered them £1million apiece to host *Slap Bang*, a more grown-up show. The lads poured cold water on the telephone-number salaries that the press suggested they were being offered. But the direction their careers were moving in slowly emerged.

As Christmas 2001 loomed, news began leaking out that their departure from the Saturday morning kids' show *SM:tv Live* loomed large. After three and a half years hosting the show, Ant and Dec were nearing the end of the road as children's presenters. Jokes about Ant's 'Frankenstein' forehead were beginning to be a running gag on the show – this joke was nothing to do with horror films or Ant's head shape, it was more a dig at his receding hairline. Clearly the two lads, and the producers and agents behind them, felt that it was time for them to move on. Time for them to come of age and do something different.

Saturday 1 December 2001 proved a massive turning point for the Tyneside Two. Their last ever *SM:tv Live* signalled their departure for pastures new. Now, for the first time, they were able watch the show in bed at home, enjoying a lie-in to nurse their hangovers from the night before – like other viewers.

Other programmes followed, notably the hit show *Pop Idol*, which featured Ant and Dec as presenters and roving reporters, chatting to contestants who were vying to become Britain's favourite new pop sensation. On many occasions during the series, Ant and Dec earned sympathy from viewers at home by siding with the contestants, rather than their critical judges. Also before Christmas there was *Record of the Year*, an ITV evening show setting out to select the nation's top chart hit from the past 12 months. While this show cast Ant and Dec more in the style of their own *cd:uk*, in which they'd introduce the latest pop singles to the nation every Saturday morning after *SM:tv Live*, their *Pop Idol* roles put them in a new light – as more mature presenters, attracting perhaps a slightly older audience.

But there was one instantly noticeable difference between the primetime *Record of the Year* and the *cd:uk* series. Groomed behind the scenes by their agents and ITV's costume department, the brightly lit and colourful Saturday morning kids' show featured Ant and Dec wearing jazzy open-necked shirts and sporty outfits; but on the evening show the lighting was far more subdued, and the presenters both wore super-smart, professionally tailored dark suits. Dec even sported a white handkerchief in his breast pocket – a conventional touch that would have been welcome in a Pall Mall gentlemen's club.

The change of career direction signalled exciting times for the pair of them – but Ant and Dec were overcome with emotion when the time came for them to bow out of *SM:tv Live*. Their last show was a tearful affair.

'The whole decision to leave was quite gut-wrenching,' Dec admitted the week after they left the series. 'Doing the last show was very upsetting. They [the producers and researchers] didn't tell us what was going to go on or who the guests were, so the whole thing was a big surprise for us. We miss it already but we're hugely excited about the next year.

'I'll miss the relationship with Cat [Deeley, their co-host]. The three of us get on really well. We have really good chemistry and we enjoy working together. We'll stay friends but I'll miss that working relationship. Cat's great to work with, great fun to be around – and she's lush as well!

'We've had a great time on *SM:tv Live*, really happy times – the happiest of my professional life so far. It's going to be hard to top that.'

Ant agrees, adding with genuine sincerity, 'We are also very proud of the unique relationship we have with our viewers. We hope they will come with us to whatever we do next.'

Ant found it 'gut wrenching' to quit *SM:tv* for different reasons ... If you thought it was only because he felt nostalgic about missing the show, think again! He was also thinking of his

'The whole decision to leave was quite gut-wrenching'

stomach!

'I've had the same egg mayo baguette every Friday for the last three and a half years,' he confessed. Aw!

So what is next for these two rising stars? And why has the spotlight lingered so long and brightly upon them?

It makes you wonder, by the time the Royal Variety Performance rolls round in the year 2012, who will be left to star in the line-up. Will the industry's elder statesmen and women of today – veterans like Bruce Forsyth, Cilla Black, Michael Parkinson, Bob Monkhouse and Des O'Connor – still be around? Or will they have gracefully retired by then? More to the point, Ant and Dec are *already* beginning to upstage their elders, and it's the younger generation of stars who are going to capture the attention of audiences in the future.

The establishment already recognises the young pretenders' talents and future prospects. ITV certainly does. They have recently struck a new deal with Ant and Dec, reportedly for £2million, which sees the duo returning to our screens with a new primetime Saturday evening show, a one-hour programme that will attract more of a family audience than just kids. 'It's a big step. We'll just have to suck it and see,' Dec ventured rather nervously in December as plans for the new series were being worked out.

At one stage during the making of *Pop Idol*, one of the judges, record industry guru and veteran producer Pete Waterman, briefly entertained the idea of trying to lure Ant and Dec into making a return to their music careers. He offered to take them back into the recording studio, but the boys would have none of it. They felt they had served their time as pop stars and wanted to move forward. Recently though there have reportedly been many offers to star in sitcoms and big-screen films ...

Between them, Ant and Dec have already notched up an enormous amount of experience in the entertainment industry. Amazingly, it totals nearly a quarter of a century, and much of their experience has been gained in front of the cameras during *live* programmes – something of a rarity these days, when so much television is pre-recorded and edited.

Ant and Dec's live blunders make great television – and they know it. The times when they have genuinely dropped clangers are actually fairly far and few between. And when something does go disastrously wrong on the studio floor, their quick-witted reaction and split-second comedy timing often rescues the situation. This is one of the reasons why they are such a star turn. When their guests mess up their lines, it's even funnier. Ant and Dec often say that their fans tell them they love it when mistakes happen on air. Live television is all about making the best of those situations and capitalising on them.

As we all know, there are plenty of presenters who seem to struggle reading the autocue. But Ant and Dec's experience has given them enormous confidence on camera, which in turn means that we can relax in their company. Just how did this innate confidence come about? Where and when did their remarkable story begin? For the answers we must journey to Tyneside and back to a time long before the living memory of their current fans.

It all began just as the Vietnam War was coming to an end, when legendary British racing driver Graham Hill was tragically killed in an air crash, and when everyone was raving about Hollywood actor Jack Nicholson, who starred that year in the film called *One Flew Over The Cuckoo's Nest*. That year – the year it all began for Ant and Dec – was 1975.

Far away from glitzy Hollywood, in the north of England, one flew over the cuckoo's nest for real up on Tyneside. It was the Stork, and in her big yellow beak hung two tiny linen bundles containing a pair of spiky-haired Geordie babies. As the big bird flew, the two babies slept soundly in blankets patterned with black and white stripes, perfectly matching the world-famous Newcastle United strip. The big bird hovered over a housing estate, then adjusted her wings to begin circling, and finally made her descent …

Rejoice: the Baby Geordies!

Declan Joseph Oliver Donnelly was born into a sprawling Irish Roman Catholic family on 25 September 1975. For his mam Anne, who worked as a housekeeper, and dad Alphonsus, retired, bonny baby Declan was lucky Number Seven, joining his six elder brothers and sisters at the Donnelly family home on the Cruddas Park estate in Newcastle's West End.

The eldest of Dec's three sisters, Patricia, was 12 when he was born, so Dec was in safe hands. All the children enjoyed helping mam look after the new arrival. And still today, the kids – that's sisters Patricia, now 37, Moira, 31 and Camalia, 27, and brothers Eamonn, 36, Martin, 35 and Dermott, 32 – all remain a close-knit clan.

Anne and Alphonsus had moved into their modest £10,000 council house in 1968, seven years before Dec was born, so the kids had already made loads of friends in the neighbourhood and young Declan soon fitted in well.

When baby Dec was just eight weeks old and still gurgling in his cot, something amazing happened that was to change his life for ever. One frosty evening in November, his eyes twinkled as he lay there, perhaps sensing a fleeting moment of magic was passing in the night. Baby Dec couldn't put his little pudgy finger on it, he couldn't explain what it was. What's more, this mysterious and monumental event was to remain cloaked and hidden from him for a further 13 years.

Had a bright star crossed the sky? No. Were three robed strangers bearing gifts heading his way? No way, mon!

In truth, less than a mile down the road in a neighbouring district of Newcastle, a family gathering bore witness to the birth of another Geordie baby, welcomed to the world by gasps of delight from his mam Christine and dad Raymond.

Baby Anthony David McPartlin bounced into this world on 18 November 1975. And at the family's three-bedroomed council house home in Fenham, Newcastle, the celebrations began.

Ant's mam, Christine, who works as a beautician, was overjoyed by the birth. So, too, of course, was his dad, a plumber by trade. Nowadays, Ant says, his mam is so star-struck by her successful son that whenever the gas man comes to call she loves to hand out signed photos of Ant and natter on about all the things he's done and places he's been.

But let's spare Ant's blushes and return to the Donnelly household.

Entry to the main school was set at age four but in 1978, at the age of three, Dec became a pupil at St Michael's Roman Catholic Primary School in Elswick, Newcastle. He joined the nursery where he made friends quickly and remains, to this day, one of the school's favourite 'old boys'. Dec's niece and nephew are pupils there now.

As his fourth and fifth birthdays flew by, Dec would be out after school, playing football with his chums or climbing trees – a favourite pastime. He also liked to zoom round the streets on his bike, and his love of life in the fast lane was clearly apparent by the age of six – when he was injured in a spectacular bike crash. He fell off and bit through his tongue.

As the youngest in his family, Dec soon became, by his own admission, 'a bit of a show-off'. Every Christmas the family would egg him on and beg him to give them a song. He would always respond by performing a number or two, and being the centre of attention quickly grew on him. It also gave the young lad early confidence that was to prove so vital later on. Dermott, Dec's elder brother, recalls, 'Declan was the youngest, so he got a lot of attention. That's where he got the idea of being a showman. He performed for us first. We would egg him on doing breakdancing and that.'

After primary school Dec joined St Cuthbert's High School on West Road, Newcastle, an all-boys Catholic ex-grammar school. Other famous 'old boys' from the school include rock star Sting, football manager Lawrie McMenemy and Neil Tennant from the Pet Shop Boys. As his studies progressed, Dec was like most of the others in his class. He dreamed only of becoming a professional footballer. But his talents were to kick him in a different direction.

When he sat his GCSEs, Dec notched up three Bs, two Cs, a D and two Fs for art and physics. One school report read, 'Must try harder!' He did.

These days, Dec prides himself on his appearance and likes to spend some of his earnings on clothes. He's well known to his fans as a trendy dresser. One of his earliest recollections is an early indicator of the fashion-conscious image he enjoys today. When he was a small boy his mam bought him a pair of bright yellow trousers and Dec hated wearing them. He claims he even wet himself on purpose once – just so he could get out of having to put them on.

Ant also has a funny story about the clothes he had to wear as a schoolboy. Ant was a pupil at Wingrove Junior School, where he endured one of his most embarrassing moments ever. His Nan packed him off to school one morning when aged six, wearing a natty pair of pink Y-fronts. She'd bought them for him in a pack of three at Marks & Sparks and, on the day Ant was forced to put them on, he had PE. He didn't have the proper gym kit to wear and the teacher insisted he go through with the lesson in his pink Y-fronts in front of all his classmates. Ant had to suffer this despite his attempts to feign a leg injury, which failed to impress anyone.

By now, Ant was catching up with Dec on the sibling front. Ant had a sister, Sarah, three years younger than him. But he had to wait a few more years before his other sister, Emma, came into the world. Emma is now aged 10.

Young Ant was growing up fast and he reckoned it was time to get some work. His first ever job was as a paperboy and he remembers his first wage packet – £6.20.

'It sounded quite a lot at the time,' he reflects over a decade later. ' But it meant getting up really early and I was always scared, at least at first, of putting the wrong papers through the wrong doors! One good thing about the job was free papers, if you know what I mean!!'

Ant graduated to Rutherford Comprehensive, now Westgate Community College, 'a comprehensive with girls', as Ant puts

13

it. The school took 11- to 18-year-olds and, like all schools for that age group, concentrated on helping teenagers achieve success in their exams. But from the very beginning of his schooldays, Ant wanted only to be an actor.

He did achieve decent exam results though ... 'I got two Bs, two Cs, two Ds and an E. Not bad – I wasn't there much!' Ant jokes.

One of his school reports reads, 'Anthony is very easily distracted and could be OK if only he applied himself properly.'

While Declan was applying himself to his school studies, he was for a time distracted by other influences that were every bit as important – even though they were nothing to do with classrooms, teachers or homework. Before Dec reached his teens, he had formed a particularly close bond with Dermott, who is seven years his senior. 'Dermott's the next brother up from me, so he was quite an influence,' Declan reflected in an interview years later.

'At the time I was growing up, I'd tell him what I thought and he'd listen.'

Both boys remember learning in school about CAFOD, the Catholic Agency For Overseas Development.

But, although the two brothers share deep religious convictions to this day, they parted company when it came to choosing a career. At first they both seriously considered joining the priesthood, as Dec admitted in a rare and revealing interview he gave to *CAFOD Magazine* in 1997. Under the headline 'The pop star and the priest', Dec talked openly for the first time about his religious beliefs, and his admiration for his elder brother, who did go on to take holy orders.

'The Donnelly brothers from Newcastle may not seem to have a lot in common. Dermott, 29, is a priest in the youth mission team of Hexham and Newcastle Diocese ... The other shares a London bachelor pad with his TV co-star. But the two lads admit there is more to each of them than meets the eye.'

'Religion is still a major thing for me,' declares Dec. 'Although I've moved to London and I share a flat with Ant now, I've still got two crucifixes in my room and a bottle of water from Lourdes next to my bed.'

'The pop star and the priest'

Dec told *The Times* he remains a practising Catholic. 'I pray all the time. I still go to Mass. I went to confession a couple of weeks ago. I never really talk about this. I don't really want to sound American and wanky about it.'

Dec revealed that when Dermott went off to study for the priesthood, it was something he, too, considered as a career. 'It was something I thought I could do and maybe I should do. I was discovering religion and reading through the Bible and thinking about things. But I went through the process and realised I couldn't do it. That's why I've a lot of admiration and respect for our priests. It's a great skill to have to be on call for all those people and bringing that message. But it wasn't the right thing for me to do – I had to go and be a pop star instead!'

Only a few years later, Declan started appearing in the BBC children's teatime drama *Byker Grove* and fame was just around the corner. It launched his TV and pop career, with work often luring him away from the Northeast. But over the years, the brothers have remained close. 'My best characteristic is that I'm calm and balanced,' says Declan.

15

'I'm a Libran and always try to avoid an argument. If I do get unbalanced, I have a right grump – especially in the mornings.'

Dermott agrees. 'Declan can be stroppy,' he says. Despite that, Declan's level-headed attitude, that 'calm and balanced' nature, as he puts it, and Ant's streetwise, no-nonsense approach to life, are qualities that were to stand them both in good stead in the years to come.

They hadn't met each other yet, of course. But as each boy grew up, nurtured towards their teens by their loving and supportive families, their strong characters were being built and two distinctive personalities were emerging. Deep within them, both boys were determined to make something of their lives. At which precise age they realised they were different in some way from their peers remains unknown. But soon, as events were to overtake them, one thing became clear – neither Ant nor Dec was going to tread the same pathway as the majority of their classmates.

The other lads were going on to become painters and decorators, chippies and plasterers, working on Newcastle's housing estates. As grown men, now in their mid-20s just like Ant and Dec, these classroom contemporaries are working as labourers and minicab drivers today. But fate held something rather different in store for our two Geordie youngsters. They were too young to grasp the notion of celebrity, but the rebel in each of them was to guarantee that they would make their mark. They were sure of that.

In their own individual ways, they both enjoyed showing off, being the centre of attention, standing out from the crowd. And soon enough they were going to have their chance to show the world what they could do.

Early Signs of Talent

As they approached their teenage years, fresh-faced Geordie lads Anthony McPartlin and Declan Donnelly studied hard at school, kept their noses clean and didn't get into any serious trouble, unlike some of the other kids in their neighbourhood.

But their sudden switch to the fast lane, plucked from obscurity in the classroom to local hero status as stars of the region's most famous, high-profile TV series *Byker Grove*, was truly remarkable – considering the tough social background from which they emerged.

Declan was raised on the notorious Cruddas Park council estate in Newcastle's West End, where petty crime was rife, according to one local clergyman who got to know Dec well in his youth. Burglary, drug dealing, mugging and joyriding were all commonplace in the area, where some pretty rough diamonds roamed the streets, often recruiting local children to become involved in the crime scene.

Church of England vicar George Curry has lived in the area for over 20 years. He ran a very successful, friendly and well-attended youth club at St Stephen's Church in Clumber Street, a short walk from Dec's home. Dec was a fresh-faced teenager when he first began spending his Friday nights there, chumming up with the two dozen or so other 11- to 18-year-olds who also flocked to the church hall to play pool, table tennis and seven-a-side football.

'Unfortunately the West End has a dreadful history of criminality,' George Curry recalls. 'Crime rates were very high. At that time, it had the highest social deprivation for the north of England. Burglary was a major crime, mugging was also a big problem. We had ladies who had their handbags taken. There were sadly people around who were into crime, the joyriders, the drug addicts, the drug pushers. There was thieving and a lot of burglary and many children were used in these things.'

'There's always peer group pressure but Declan didn't give in.'

'I used to walk round and see people not far from where Declan was living, having their fixes of cannabis and all the rest. Drugs have been a major problem. There have been dealers in houses and on the streets in that area. There were regular raids by the police, too, both in the flats and in the houses at that time – and it's still going on. Joyriders were pretty active on Cambridge Street and Park Road, which are adjacent to the street where Dec's family live, near the tower blocks.'

The social context in which Declan made a success of his life makes his achievements all the more heartening and uplifting, says George. 'There's always peer group pressure but Declan didn't give in. An area gets a name and Cruddas Park housing estate has got a name. But Declan was a clean-living boy. He was aware of what was happening but kept himself away from it.'

In fact Dec has admitted that, in one daft moment out of character, he once stole some balloons from a shop. But he says he felt so bad about what he'd done that he took them straight back. His honesty after the event was a sure sign that here was a lad who was made of sterner stuff than some of his contemporaries.

'He was not exactly the same as the typical West End child. Here was a lad who had a sense of right and wrong, had a degree of maturity about him from the emotional point of view, and stability,' adds George.

'Dec was obviously, at home and at school, taught moral values – and they came across. Here was a guy who was not into the crime that many others were into.'

Ant was also born in Newcastle's West End, and, according to his school teachers, he too did well – against the odds.

Geoff Younger was head of year at Rutherford Comprehensive School when an 11-year-old McPartlin, or Anthony, as he was known at school, joined the first year in 1987. Anthony spent five years there, and as a sixth former returned aged 16 to prepare for his exams, which included media studies.

19

But Anthony stayed in the sixth form for only a few weeks before he decided to concentrate on his acting career. His studies were interrupted by his recruitment into the cast of *Byker Grove*. Taking stock of his future and weighing up his priorities, Anthony decided he'd rather spend his time on the *Byker Grove* set than at school. He preferred to be poring over his TV scripts rather than his school books.

Mr Younger, a smartly-dressed, silver-haired man with a friendly smile, is now assistant principal at the college. He told me, 'Anthony came across as a keen and enthusiastic lad. He was well presented and I always remember that his mam was keen for him to do well at school. The family lived just round at the back of the school. You could see his house from the school buildings, only a few minutes walk across the back field. With him living so close to school he may have been tempted to play truant – but he didn't. He was a well accepted, friendly, nice lad within the year group. He just got on with things as they presented themselves.

'Perhaps I wouldn't have put him down to be going into showbusiness. He didn't come across as somebody who wanted to be on the stage. He came over as an average type of lad who obviously enjoyed life and enjoyed hanging around with his mates. If there was a bit of tomfoolery going on in the classroom, he would get involved with it, along with the majority of others. But that was just pranks in the classroom, a touch of naughtiness.

Years later, on *SM:tv Live*, Ant was being tested by another young contestant during the Challenge Ant section where each week a youngster attempted to beat Ant in a general knowledge quiz. Ant was asked, 'Where is the smallest bone in the human body?' and he replied, correctly, 'In your ear.'

'He's been like a flower, bud-like at school and then blossoming after he left. Anthony will always be welcome back to his old school as a guest. We promise to roll out the red carpet for him!'

Another teacher, Ken Bartle, who taught Anthony science, was less than impressed with his former pupil's academic prowess — and he got in touch with Ant by e-mail to say so!

Everyone in the studio was surprised that Ant had managed to get the answer right because he had often been defeated by questions on science subjects like human biology, maths and the solar system. As an encouragement to any kids considering applying to Challenge Ant themselves, Dec even told viewers

watching the programme at home, 'If you want to beat Ant, kids, just ask him a maths question!'

All this failed to impress Anthony's former science teacher Mr Bartle. He'd been watching the programme and he fired off an e-mail to the studio to express his tongue-in-cheek disappointment at discovering how little Ant had remembered from his science lessons. Mr Bartle's e-mail was read out live on air – much to Ant's embarrassment, and to the enjoyment of millions of viewers.

The two boys may not have excelled in science classes at school, but they both had their heads screwed on the right way. And Dec was the first of the pair to show early signs of ambition. By the late 1980s young Declan, who had just reached his teens, was already very focused on his career. In Newcastle he sought out artists' agent Dave Holly, who remembers the fresh-faced young man walking into his office, pulling out his Filofax, and wanting to talk business from the word go.

This amazingly mature behaviour from someone so inexperienced proved a certain indicator that here was a fresh talent keen to get ahead – a young man with firmly fixed notions about his own future. Although he was little more than a boy, he already had a steely determination to grow up fast and 'make it' in the precarious world of showbusiness.

Ant also proved early on that he was different from his peers. With his confident air and sense of 'attitude' towards life in general, he impressed his drama teacher at school, who decided to put him up for an audition on a local TV show.

The kids show, *Why Don't You?* was a favourite among Ant's classmates and he became an instant hit at school after winning the part. For his audition, Ant performed a sketch where he pretended to be an old man driving a bus. The talent scouts were duly impressed and Ant got the job.

Stardom beckoned, and back in the school corridors Ant's mates would tease him by singing the *Why Don't You?* theme tune whenever he walked by. But Ant didn't care he was on his way. He had a toe-hold.

Soon enough, both Ant and Dec were to be plucked from school to sample a very different lifestyle to the one to which they were accustomed. For the budding talents of both Declan and Anthony were due to find expression in a brand new television series set, conveniently for them, in the heart of their home city of Newcastle. What a gift! They had no idea what lay in store for them, but it was their big chance to show the world what they could do, an opportunity for the two teenagers to let their talents and ambitions blossom.

In a nutshell, the BBC launch was to change these two young lads' lives beyond recognition. And for ever.

Whey Aye, Welcome to the Lads

4

As we have seen, Ant and Dec's families lived about a mile apart and the two boys grew up less than 10 minutes away from each other's homes. But the McPartlins and the Donnellys never knew each other and the two youngsters didn't meet until they were both cast in the award-winning series set in a fictional Newcastle youth club, *Byker Grove*.

Dec was aged 13 when he joined the cast for the programme's first series. Episode one was screened on 8 November 1989 – and since then, more than 4,000 young people from the Northeast have appeared in the series. The show's hugely talented and experienced producer at the time, Matthew Robinson, is now head of drama at BBC Wales in Cardiff. Matthew, who went on after *Byker Grove* to become executive producer at *EastEnders*, has also worked on episodes of *Brookside*, *Coronation Street* and *Emmerdale*. Cambridge University graduate Matthew was at the helm for over 200 *Byker Grove* episodes, overseeing nine series of the show – which, looking back, he now regards as one of the most exciting chapters in his career.

The twice-weekly BBC series became a cult for the five-million-plus viewers who tuned in regularly. The children's soap was a huge hit – and everyone associated with the show knew it.

Having worked with some of the biggest stars in the business, Matthew Robinson can certainly spot talent when he sees it. And discovering Ant and Dec is one of his proudest achievements. He vividly remembers the day Dec rang up to say he'd heard that *Byker Grove* was happening and asked to audition. Young Dec had seen an advert in the local newspaper saying the BBC was on the hunt for young actors, and had been egged on by his mam, Anne, who had prompted him to apply for a screen test.

'He had a tremendous amount of precocious, childhood charm – and he knew it. He's still got it today,' Matthew remembers fondly. 'It was pretty clear to me from the moment I met him that he had star quality. He was 12 coming on 13 at the time. Declan had something special. It was his eyes and his character that made him stand out from all the others he was competing with. I didn't have anyone in the show at the time who was quite like him. I thought he would catch the audience's imagination in a great way. I snapped him up.

'He always wanted to be a star – that was clear from the start. It wasn't, however, our intention to have him as one of the main players to begin with. He started off with a bit part and then he just took off. And so we started to write the scripts around him and brought him more and more to the front. He deserved the big storylines. Something happened to him over the next two to three years. He was a very good-looking and wonderful lad, and his appeal to the females was incredible.'

'He always wanted to be a star'

Dec clearly remembers the adrenaline surge of his first few weeks. His new *Byker Grove* contract was his first proper job. 'I remember the nervous excitement of those first few weeks – and the real sense of growing up,' he reflects.

Since the show began, the Mitre has been the location of the *Byker Grove* youth centre. It's a Victorian mansion and former pub, set in three acres of Benwell, a Newcastle suburb. The Mitre was bought by the BBC in 1990 and is an all-purpose studio, with sets, production offices, make-up and wardrobe departments, restrooms, canteens and even a classroom, where young members of the cast who are away from school can catch up with their homework whenever they are not required on set.

When Ant joined the cast for the second series, Dec recalls spotting him one day, sitting in a corner with his head in his hands. His face was a misery and Dec thought he was upset about something – nowadays, Dec knows better, of course. That's just Ant's face!

Dec likes to recall that in later years, when the twosome were pop stars on the road, girl fans would sometimes ask him to get Ant's autograph for them – because they were too nervous of Ant, who looked so cheesed off.

When Ant first met Dec on the set of *Byker Grove*, they were both aged 13 but they didn't become instant friends. Dec had already been in the first series, so he thought he was the bee's knees. A few weeks later, they started talking and struck up a rapport. Ant says they only became best mates after they'd been to watch Newcastle play. 'I thought he was cheeky then and now I love his sense of humour,' he says.

For *Byker Grove*, Ant was first spotted by Matthew Robinson's colleague, production manager Andy Snelgrove. Matthew would receive hundreds of letters from children who were desperate to become members of the cast. But the number that could be taken on by the show was limited because the cast needed regular characters. Talent scouts from the series regularly trawled schools in the area, asking teachers if there were any youngsters who were keen to audition. Ant came to light when Andy contacted his school, Rutherford Comprehensive. Andy was struck by Ant's personality and invited him to audition for the show.

Ant, of course, had already gained some experience of TV, working on *Why Don't You?*, but that day his life was to change for ever. This was his ticket to ride – and he grabbed it with both hands.

Ant was originally cast in the role of Robert, a disabled lad who'd had an accident playing football. His wheelchair-bound character was dropped only a couple of days before filming began. That's when he was cast as PJ, a streetwise DJ who went on, with his mate Duncan, to form a band, a duo named Groove Matrix. From the outset, Dec was a natural, and at rehearsals it became clear that Ant's role was also perfectly suited to his personality.

'It wasn't very long before his character developed into someone who was always joking and playing pranks,' adds Matthew candidly. 'By the time they reached 13 and 14 it was clear they had something very special, and everything just went mad. Sackloads of mail started to arrive for them; the post for those two was miles above anyone else's. It was very satisfying for us – we had two stars.'

Ant and Dec – and their alter egos, best friends PJ and Duncan – were hugely popular. 'The office was inundated with fan mail,' recalls one former *Byker Grove* script editor, Simon Heath. 'They were in a show where they were pretty much playing themselves. It was clear they had winning personalities and a naturalness in front of the camera.'

As they moved into their teens, Ant and Dec's new-found fame also gave them their first taste of what it felt like to be mobbed by fans – fans who were almost obsessed with getting close to their new idols.

They presented a programme on Tyneside called *Gimme 5* which was co-presented by family favourite Jenny Powell for four years from 1991. It was a series that helped them cut their broadcasting teeth and it also provided them with a dedicated following. But Ant was in two minds about the fans. 'We'd arrive and there'd be girls waiting outside in the freezing weather, their lips blue and their fingers icy cold. You want to say, "Don't do this for me, go home and sit in the warm." On the other hand, knowing that people will go to those extremes to see you is flattering, you can't deny that.'

A successful, exciting new partnership had been forged on *Byker Grove* – and this new dynamic duo of PJ and Duncan was to carry on winning fans for years to come. They were to win countless awards – although few people surrounding them at that time suspected what lay in store for the two young talents.

'We'd arrive and there'd be girls waiting outside in the freezing weather, their lips blue and their fingers icy cold.'

Part of the appeal of *Byker Grove*, which in Ant and Dec's day drew between four and five million viewers, is its fearless approach to tackling controversial issues that are usually avoided by children's television producers and scriptwriters. Teenage sex and pregnancy, child abuse, drugs, petty and violent crime, religious cults, terminal illness, bullying, joyriding, coming to terms with disability and homosexuality – all are topics that have been dramatised realistically and sensitively. Addressing these issues in gritty storylines has won the series respect among its audience – and also a cluster of awards. It became one of television's biggest success stories of the 1990s.

At one point the Broadcasting Standards Council, the television watchdog, was asked to adjudicate after viewers complained about a scene in which a boy was seen preparing for a night out by buying condoms. The BSC found in the programme's favour.

When Ant started work at *Byker Grove* he'd just turned 13 and, looking back now on those early days, he is surprisingly grateful for the discipline he learned from working on a professional and high profile series. Giggling fits on set were banned because every member of the cast was reminded that time was money (and the licence-payers' money too). Actors were warned that if they larked about they would get booted off the show.

The discipline Ant learned on the *Byker Grove* set stood him in good stead when he returned to school at Rutherford Comprehensive, where he continued for a while. Despite his new-found fame, Ant never bragged about his acting career or his celebrity status, according to his teachers at the time.

'He had a lot of time off to do *Byker Grove*,' one of Ant's former schoolmasters told me. 'But when he came back to class he was never blasé or over the top with the fame he had achieved. I have to say that about the lad. He didn't come in bragging. He was living in a council house at the end of the street, and I dare say money hadn't been abundant. Although I don't know what the conditions are on pay, being a star he would have been on some decent money. But he never came in flashing it about or throwing it around.'

At the church youth club where Dec was a regular, even the vicar noticed the attention he was getting. 'Declan was a handsome young man and there were girls who obviously found him attractive,' according to the Reverend George Curry. 'You would hear comments and observe. Girls at that stage are giggly and bubbly and they like sharing together. You could hear the comments from time to time and it was obvious that here was someone involved in television programmes, a handsome young lad. But Declan had a quiet, solid and modest personality. When he was 14,15 and 16 he joined in with everyone but I wouldn't have said he was an effervescent personality. I never got the impression he was ambitious. There was always a gentleness, a self-effacing, humble side to Declan which I was impressed with as an individual. I thought, this lad is different from so many others in the West End.'

Sometimes, Declan brought along *Byker Grove* books to the youth club, outlining stories from the series. Other kids at the club also brought them, and would ask Declan to autograph them.

'He was a budding TV celebrity and he used to talk about the filming at the Mitre, which decades ago, before the BBC took it over, had been the former Bishop of Newcastle's residence. By this time, Declan had been on *Byker Grove* for some while and the others were intrigued. He was still at school but he fitted in well. He wasn't like some of the lads, whose every other word began with an F. He was there rubbing shoulders with them but he never caused any trouble.

George Curry recalled that one of young Declan's favourite ways of passing the time was to play pool. He was a nifty player, too. 'He was regularly round the table and I had a few games with him. Mind you, he always beat me,' the vicar chuckles.

Dec may have been largely unaffected by fame in his early years but there were others whose lives were to be transformed the moment they appeared in *Byker Grove*. Another former cast member who quickly went on to establish a career in showbusiness is TV presenter and actress Donna Air. The Gosforth-bred star, who played cheeky little Charlie in the series, starred in *Byker Grove* from the age of 11 until she was 15. These days she is based in London, but she has never forgotten her roots and is very much a Geordie at heart.

Ant and Dec were having the time of their lives. They had been cast in a high profile BBC series and for the first time in their lives their friends were treating them like celebrities. They could hardly believe their luck. They had instant street cred and they were recognised wherever they went.

But as the weeks turned into months, and then years, and the series rolled by, Ant and Dec began to realise that one thing was working against them – their ages. Soon, they approached the upper age limit for cast members, the middle to upper teens.

Both Ant and Dec were gutted when the time came for them to leave the drama. They didn't want to move on. When they did, though, they went out in style, with a bang, leaving in the wake of one of the series' most dramatic ever storylines. PJ, played by Ant, was blinded in a paint-balling accident and went to a blind school, and Duncan left with him to be a helper.

It had been five years since Ant first appeared on *Byker Grove*. When he left, he enrolled to study a BTEC in performing arts. He was planning to apply for drama school in London, and hoped to find more work as an actor.

Dec was 18 at the time. On one of the last days on the set, Matthew came running after them as they were leaving. He said there was a record company producer on the phone who wanted to offer them a recording contract. The boys thought he was joking, but a few days later their agent also telephoned and, to their amazement, he confirmed the news. They could hardly believe it.

They say that truth is stranger than fiction – and what was happening to Ant and Dec was indisputable proof that the age old saying is true. In the fictional, make-believe world of *Byker Grove*, screen characters PJ and Duncan may have been bowing out of the series. But in real life, to the delight of their fans in the outside world, their pop careers were only just beginning.

Discography

Britain's most famous Geordie pop stars have to date produced three albums plus a compilation LP and 14 hit singles. Here's a list of their chart successes:

Albums:

1994: Psyche

1995: Top Katz

1997: The Cult of Ant and Dec

2001: Ant and Dec: The Greatest Hits Album

Singles:

1993: Tonight I'm Free

1994: Why Me?, Let's Get Ready to Rhumble, If I Give You My Number, Eternal Love

1995: Our Radio Rocks, Stuck on You, U Krazy Katz, Perfect

1996: Stepping Stone, Better Watch Out, When I Fall in Love

1997: Shout, Falling

Byker Grove Bits

1   *Byker Grove* has been sold to 13 countries including the Czech Republic, Iceland, Lebanon, Saudi Arabia and Zambia.

2   In an average year of production, the actors speak 800,000 words during rehearsals and recordings.

3   It's thirsty work – between them the cast and crew devour 8,500 rolls and 30,000 cups of tea per series.

4   The Mitre, where the series is filmed, is reputed to be haunted by a ghost.

5   In 1993, according to 'eyewitness' reports, the ghost moved from the costume department to the ladies' toilets. Watch out, girls!

6   In 1993, PJ's screen mum was played by Ant's *real* Mum, Christine.

7   The show hit the headlines in 1994 when it featured a controversial gay kiss between two male actors aged just 16 and 17. Parents bombarded the BBC with complaints but seven million viewers still tuned in to watch the scene.

8   One Tory MP called the programme 'disgraceful', another MP branded the scene 'distasteful'. The lobby group Christian Voice claimed the BBC was 'thoroughly irresponsible' for showing the kiss.

9   Other previously unknown Geordie youngsters who found fame after *Byker* include Casper Berry, who played Gil in the first two series. He headed for Hollywood after launching his debut feature film *Down Time*.

10 *Byker Grove* celebrated its 10th birthday with a huge party in November 1998.

31

From Byker to Hitchhiker: Donna's a Rising Star

onna, now a star and peak-time video-jockey at MTV, had a crack at the pop charts after she left *Byker Grove* just like Ant and Dec. Her pop group Crush had a handful of hits in Britain and she toured Asia, America and Japan with the band. Donna also developed her acting career and starred as a prostitute in Lynda La Plante's drama *Supply and Demand*, then opted for a change of image when she took on a new role in Catherine Cookson's *A Dinner of Herbs*. Her film work includes *The Mummy Returns* and *Still Crazy*, in which Donna plays a Dutch hitchhiker alongside Billy Connolly. Her TV presenting break came with MTV's *Select* programme and later with Channel 4's *Popgun* and *Apocalypse Now*, but today Donna is best known for fronting Channel 4's *The Big Breakfast*.

Bye-Bye Byker

5

A storyline in their hit BBC series *Byker Grove*, inspired by chance one day after its producer tuned into a local radio station, sparked a major turning point in Ant and Dec's budding careers.

Suddenly and unexpectedly, the duo were to find themselves embarking on a four-year, three-album teeny-pop career and being catapulted to fame and fortune as heart-throb pop idols. As the unsuspecting teenagers quietly went about their routine daily rehearsals on the Tyneside kids' drama, they had no idea that fate was about to strike – or what lay waiting for them just around the corner.

As the summer of 1993 loomed, within months they were to wave goodbye to their *Byker Grove* colleagues and their low-key lifestyle on Tyneside. Before long newspapers and magazines would be posting their photos on front pages and describing them as 'Britain's best-selling pop duo'. Globetrotting tours loomed, with trips to far-flung places like the Far East, Australia and Japan – countries they had studied in geography classes at school but never dreamt they would visit.

Oh – and one other major surprise was in store. Girls.

Byker Grove had brought both lads a degree of adulation and respect from their peers and school chums. But now, as their careers relaunched into the crazy world of pop, that was to change. Before, they had been admired – now they were to become *idolised* by their fans, who would stalk their movements, ambush them at their hotels and hurl their underwear on stage at every opportunity.

Matthew Robinson, *Byker Grove*'s producer and creator, a veteran of the television and entertainment industries, is long

33

'What are we going to do with our lives?'

enough in the tooth to spot a turning point in a young star's career when he sees it. 'The real break for the pair of them came when we did the music storyline,' he told his local paper, the *Evening Chronicle*, in 1996. 'I'd been listening to the radio about how it's possible to make a record in your garage these days with all the electrical equipment available and how young lads could do it for as little as £100. Great story for *Byker Grove*, I thought.'

In *Byker Grove* the duo formed a pop group called Groove Matrix and they sang a song, written by boy band Let Loose, called *Tonight I'm Free*. When the episode was screened, *Byker Grove* fans went wild. They jammed the BBC's switchboards and swamped the show's production office with requests for copies of the record. Matthew Robinson recalls:

'*Then a phone call came in from Telstar and their music career took off. It really did happen like that, without a word of a lie. I'd hoped they would be successful, but you never know. Showbusiness is notoriously unpredictable.*'

After a phenomenal run in the BBC drama, Ant and Dec were preparing to leave *Byker Grove* in an attempt to carve a new career as pop singers. Declan remembers one night spent sitting in his £950 Mini Metro in Newcastle, worrying that no offers had arrived from record companies. 'We just sat there saying, "What are we going to do with our lives?" But we made a pact that, whatever happened, we would always be mates. We would always have each other and we would always be pals, even if everything turned tits up.'

Ant and Dec were both sad about eventually being written out of *Byker Grove*. Dec recalls, 'We were gutted – *Byker Grove* was great. I was 18 when I left. The only prospects we thought we had were getting a proper job or going back to college. We were both supposed to be studying performing arts but we never went much anyway.'

After Ant and Dec finally left *Byker Grove*, they truly landed on their feet. Suddenly, their days as PJ and Duncan, mucking around on their BMX bikes on the banks of the Tyne, were behind them. It was time to move on.

Despite this, when they launched their singing careers, they wisely decided to keep their *Byker Grove* characters' names, PJ and Duncan. Keeping the tags turned out to be a shrewd move that allowed them to build on their success as TV stars of the series. It was a canny way of making sure that their huge fan base stayed loyal and went with them when they quit the series.

But the boys' first single with music giants Telstar didn't end up doing as well as they had expected when it hit the charts. The track was released as a single just before Christmas 1994 and narrowly failed to make it into the Top 40. Still fired up with enthusiasm and excitement about their new career in the music business, the two fledgling pop idols were inspired rather than disappointed. They quickly produced a follow-up single, *Why Me?*, which made it to Number 27. Then *Let's Get Ready to Rhumble* hit Number nine. They'd made it. Pop stardom was theirs for the asking.

Later, when the pair had become established stars, Dec was gracious enough to admit that he owed a huge debt of gratitude to his first show. 'I haven't a clue where I would be today without *Byker Grove*,' he confessed. '*Byker* was our break. We had five good years there and built up a following with the audience. It was the fans and viewers who got us our record deal. They were the ones who rang the record companies to get our song released. We owe a heck of a lot to *Byker*.'

Dec seems to believe that luck played some part in his success.

'I'd hope I would always have made it into the business somehow, but I don't know how I would have got that break or what would have made me any different to the lots of other talented people out there who wanted to do it.'

As they launched their music careers on the back of the TV show, Ant, Dec and their management also knew that the average life expectancy of a pop band was three to four years. The management sent their young stars into the business with their eyes wide open, aware of the pitfalls and the pressures. Ahead of them, the duo now realised they faced one of the toughest working periods in their lives.

The lure of fame in the charts seemed pretty appealing to the two teenagers. Who wouldn't find the prospect of being idolised by crowds of young female fans attractive? But the thought of the exposure and pressures ahead was also slightly daunting.

Something else was daunting, too. Being admired so greatly and looked up to by their young fans brought its own unique pressures. Ant and Dec used to agonise over sackfuls of emotionally supercharged letters they received from girl fans who'd pour their hearts out, telling the boys their heart-wrenching stories about love, life's agonies, and various family problems.

Declan, then 19, appeared almost overcome with the emotion of it all when he spoke to journalist Jane Ridley. 'We're often asked for advice on sex and growing up. Some girls describe unhappy relationships at home or pressure from their friends to try drugs and alcohol. Their letters are just pure emotion and I'm always worrying about them. They write to us about all sorts of problems.

'Your heart goes out to them,' admitted Dec. 'Some of the fans have written to us about their home life, so we know what they are going through. When we see them, they have cheery, smiling faces but we wonder whether they're really happy underneath. You can't help but worry about people who are close to you. The fans are probably the most important people we've got at the minute.'

There was one thing that Ant and Dec had never been afraid of, however – hard work. Without more ado, they began a relentless drive to record enough songs for their first album. It meant long hours in the recording studio and a punishing

schedule. But they had learnt about discipline from Matthew Robinson on the set of *Byker Grove*, so the apprenticeship they had served at the BBC in Newcastle stood them both in good stead.

Soon, PJ and Duncan's debut album *Psyche* was released and, as their eager fans snapped it up in shops across the land, it quickly went platinum, selling more than 300,000 copies. The lads went on to scoop the 1994 Smash Hits/Radio 1 Award for Best New Act. The prestigious award was not only a feather in their caps but also amounted to a huge vote of confidence by their fans.

However, the boys' hard work wasn't confined to the recording studio. There was the UK tour to plan, and appearances on the BBC Radio 1 Roadshow, which sparked a wave of

excitement when it rolled into Whitley Bay in July 1995. There was a near riot as screaming fans greeted the former *Byker Grove* stars on their home turf. Some fans queued all night to catch a glimpse of their idols, and the crush barriers nearly buckled as hundreds of teenage girls surged forward. Their banners and placards read, 'Rhumble with Us!' and Ant and Dec duly obliged by singing their famous hit *Let's Get Ready to Rhumble*.

The following year the lads were nominated for Best Newcomer at the Brit Awards. Always ones to join in with the spirit of a high-profile star-studded occasion, Ant and Dec planned a special surprise for the paparazzi photographers who traditionally wait outside, snapping away at all the celebrities who arrive. While some bigger-name stars made grand entrances, arriving in flashy, chauffeur-driven limousines, Ant and Dec decided to be different. In a departure from all the usual pomp and ceremony, they opted to arrive in an ice-cream van. Their joke hilariously backfired when their van got stuck in heavy traffic and they arrived late. The lads leapt out all excited – only to discover that the paparazzi had gone.

Sadly, the disastrously timed ice-cream van stunt wasn't Ant and Dec's last disappointment of the night. Also nominated in their category was a new band called Oasis. And they won!

Six years later, Ant and Dec would be invited back to the Brits, this time as hosts of the awards ceremony. It was a huge honour for them to be asked to compere the event, following in the footsteps of celebrities like Chris Evans, Davina McCall and Johnny Vaughan. Acting as master of ceremonies at the event is one of the most coveted roles in television and Ant and Dec were delighted to have been offered the part. 'It's the biggest night in the British music calendar and we've always wanted to do it,' Dec admitted to journalist Karen Hockney. 'We just didn't think we'd be asked.'

Ant enthused, 'It's mega! It's one of the biggest presenting jobs you can do in British television.'

But back in 1995, as fresh-faced 20-year-old Brit Awards nominees, the honour of being asked to participate in such a prestigious ceremony clearly signalled another important milestone for the Geordie duo. As they sat there, wide-eyed, at one of the celebrity tables, they realised that the Brit Awards were – and still are – a key date in the showbusiness

establishment calendar, an event attended and keenly watched by all the entertainment industry's main movers and shakers.

For the first time in their short-lived showbusiness careers, Ant and Dec knew they had arrived – and they were here to stay. As PJ and Duncan, they had a secure future. For a while, anyway. Despite losing to Oasis, their popularity had soared to such heights that, on their UK tour, they had to hire minders to keep the fans at bay.

On the final leg of their debut tour, the hysteria and frenzy whipped up by thousands of girl fans actually left the St John Ambulance brigade with a huge headache as several of the girls fainted.

'If the success of a group was based purely on the noise generated by its followers,' pondered the Newcastle Evening Chronicle *in July 1995, 'then PJ and Duncan would be the next Beatles. The girls screamed, hugged, screamed, cried, screamed and then screamed some more.'*

Since quitting *Byker Grove* and establishing themselves as pop stars PJ and Duncan – as opposed to TV characters by those names – Ant and Dec continued to sell vast numbers of records and recruit a growing army of loyal fans.

In the guise of their teen idol pop star reincarnations, the boys had already released two hit albums. The two young Tyneside talents had also gone from strength to strength guest presenting on BBC shows like *Top of the Pops*. They were becoming an increasingly hot property in youth TV.

They'd achieved chart successes with hit singles like *Let's Get Ready to Rhumble* and *U Krazy Katz*, and had staged exhausting international tours promoting the songs. Record industry executives quickly spotted their potential, their talent and their saleability. Others paid tribute to Ant and Dec as professionals in their own right.

What the duo eventually achieved was phenomenal – 10 top 20 hits, three multi-platinum albums, 14 hit singles including *Let's Get Ready to Rhumble*, *Eternal Love* and *Our Radio Rocks*, plus two sell-out tours. But, with their careers being expertly guided by their manager Dave Holly, their success story was only just beginning.

Despite their absence from *Byker Grove*, Ant and Dec kept in constant touch with the bosses at the BBC, who watched with

interest their growing success in the pop world. After rounds of secret talks, Auntie Beeb was 'ready to rhumble' and Ant and Dec were offered their own TV series. It was to be called simply *The Ant and Dec Show*. The lads were thrilled.

The show began in April 1995 and ran for nine weeks, going out at 4.35pm on Thursday afternoons. The boys described the show as fast-moving anarchic entertainment, a cross between *Don't Forget Your Toothbrush*, hosted by Chris Evans, and *The Big Breakfast*. Another TV pundit described it as 'Larry Sanders meets *Tiswas*'. With games and gags, skits and sketches, guests and music, there was an 'anything can happen' feel to the programme, and the first edition featured Ant and Dec's hero Rolf Harris and Gladiator Panther. Other guests in later episodes included *Coronation Street* actor Ken Morley, better known as the Street's Reg Holdsworth, pop singer Sean Maguire and breakfast TV weather girl Sally Mean, who was on the verge of being offered the role of Jim Davidson's co-presenter on the BBC's *The Generation Game* on Saturday nights.

For the Geordie lads, this was an incredible opportunity they could not resist. To front their own show on TV before they'd even reached their 21st birthdays was a treat to savour.

'A few years ago, I'd have laughed my head off at the thought of someone offering us our own programme,' Ant confessed in the week before their first show went out. It was filmed in front of an audience of 120 youngsters who took part in wacky quizzes in the studio.

The show became 'the sort of thing I would have liked to have seen on telly when I was a kid,' according to Dec. 'Most of it is our warped sense of humour. By the time we have reached all of the UK population, maybe everybody will be speaking Geordie ...'

The gruelling schedule didn't seem to bother Ant, as he explained to his local paper the *Journal*, dutifully charting the career of Newcastle's two favourite sons at the time. 'The energy just seems to be there. I think we manage it all because we enjoy it. We wouldn't have dreamed of being in this position a few years ago. I'm just doing this in case my career plan to be a landscape gardener falls through.

'But seriously, we love being in the limelight and having so many people come to see us. We know that teenage stars have

In the middle of all this, Ant and Dec were offered the chance to perform for the first time in their beloved Newcastle. The sell-out show was an emotionally supercharged occasion for them both – not to mention nerve-wracking. Ant confessed to feeling 'really nervous and excited' before the concert, which marked the high-point in a UK tour. 'The rest of the tour has just been a build-up to coming home. This is probably our most important show to date, for obvious reasons. It's great to be playing to our home fans.'

Ant and Dec had actually arrived in Newcastle the day before, so that they could go and stay with their families and spend some time at home. When they got to their houses, they found hundreds of lovesick teenage girls camped outside in the street. This was approaching a Geordie equivalent of Liverpool's Beatlemania.

a limited life span, so we are just enjoying it while it lasts. At the moment, we would have to say the music was top of the list – after all, it's every kid's dream to be a pop star. But I would like to continue to work on TV in the long term.'

The ear-shattering reception Ant and Dec received from their young audience rocked the City Hall to its very foundations. A battalion of screaming youngsters thronged the hall, with 2,500 fans crammed inside and hundreds more jamming the streets outside, desperate for a glimpse of their heroes. The place went mad. On stage, the lads were bombarded with a barrage of missiles being thrown at them — everything from girls' knickers to cuddly toys and sweets.

Ant fondly remembers the fun times he shared with Declan on stage. 'Declan used to have Cadbury's Buttons thrown at him, while I used to have loads of Smarties – and it's not a nice experience having a tube of them bouncing off your head.'

In the eyes of many fans who had bought their records, the Geordie pop sensations on stage were, of course, not only their music idols but also their favourite characters from the region's best-loved TV show, *Byker Grove*. And, at this stage in their careers, Ant and Dec and their managers were not blind to the commercial potential of that dual appeal. They were still making a major impact at the box office by tapping into their screen fame as PJ and Duncan.

When they go back to Tyneside, Ant and Dec still call it home, even though they have bought their own places in London now. One of the reasons we admire them both is that their feet are still clearly very firmly on the ground. And the ground they're rooted to is their home turf in Newcastle.

When they return, they say the nicest compliments they receive from fans are not the type you'd expect – about the success they have found. The boys reckon the biggest compliment they ever get is when people turn around and say, 'You've never changed.'

Ant admits candidly, 'We don't allow ourselves to get big-headed and we always look out for each other. When we go back to Newcastle, we go out together. We love going up there because the people really keep your feet on the ground. We come from a working-class estate and were brought up not to be flash with money. Dec is very understanding and good to talk to. I'll see him down the pub and he'll always sort my problems out. But he does have this weird habit of always thinking he's only had three pints when he's actually had eight, plus a couple of bottles he drank at home.'

Having enough money to be able to go out trawling bars and restaurants with friends is a perk they have come to enjoy in the wake of their hard-earned professional success. But there is another more serious and caring side to Ant and Dec, who go out of their way to 'put something back' on Tyneside. When they visit schools and hospitals, open youth clubs and conference centres, they unashamedly use their new celebrity status to attract media attention to the region. Away from the limelight, Ant and Dec regularly help charities and children. Tyneside District Hospital in South Shields was delighted when the duo opened their new children's unit. The hospital sounded thrilled. 'The children loved Ant and Dec. They went to every bed and were charming. It was wonderful.'

Ant and Dec's input locally helps boost the profile and the fortunes of the Northeast, sometimes even helping to create jobs locally. Their fans love them for doing that. But deep in their hearts the two lads also realise that a part of them – their professional side – has moved on. They have 'come of age'. One of the great skills that they have shown so clearly over the years is their ability to 'progress', to take on board a change of image, to re-invent themselves whenever required. This way, they have been able to prolong their shelf-life as popular entertainers, whether it be it as actors, pop stars or television presenters.

Back in 1996, one such milestone change of image was in the pipeline. A fresh chapter was about to be written in their remarkable young and fast-moving careers. These were still early days and their experience as pop stars and TV presenters was still, to some degree, in its infancy, but the boys were all set to take a leap of faith – and wave goodbye to their beloved characters of PJ and Duncan for ever. They acknowledged that the roles had made them famous. They knew it was a huge risk they were taking. But it was also a calculated risk – and they had the security of knowing that they were being expertly guided by their management.

The two young lads from Tyneside had made up their minds – it was definitely time to spread their wings.

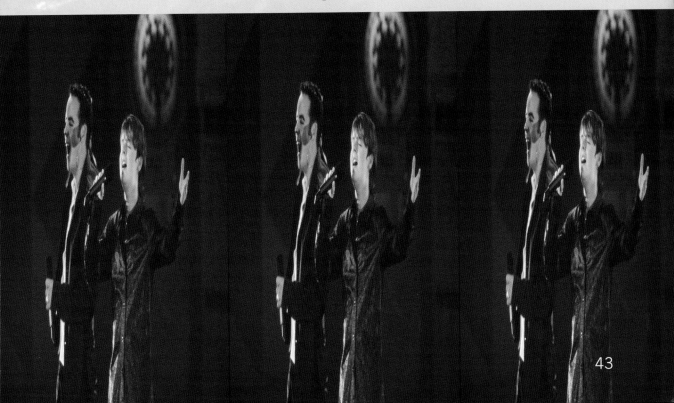

Out of the Cocoon

By the summer of 1996 both lads had waved goodbye to their teens, having recently turned 20. Between them they had already clocked up over a decade in showbusiness but, despite their early successes, it was now time for a new image.

They felt they had grown up fast, and both Ant and Dec realised that they couldn't carry on for ever in the guise of PJ and Duncan – especially as three years had now elapsed since they had left *Byker Grove*, where the characters had been 'born'. What they badly needed was a relaunch of some kind, a change of name, in fact.

They'd displayed great maturity and canniness, despite being reared in the crazy world of the teen pop idol and teen soap star. Phil Seidl, who worked with Ant and Dec at Telstar Records, told the *Mail on Sunday*, 'They were very bright. They knew exactly what they wanted to do, who they wanted to work with and how they wanted to look. They were very strong characters. They learned very quickly how to play instruments, how to write their own songs. They knew their limitations and strengths. Maybe if the TV show hadn't come along at some stage, we could have made them cheesy in the style of Steps and Wham! – you're so cheesy and naff you're cool.'

So then, their success and talent was undisputed. But the wind of change was blowing ...

The autumn of 1996 marked a crucial and telling milestone in Ant and Dec's development, both as pop stars and as TV presenters. The duo took two key, brave decisions that were to set the pace and direction of their future careers – and also earn them vital respect, not only from the public at large but also from the two industries' executives and producers.

In August '96 the boys made their big musical break. They released a new single titled *Better Watch Out* – and it was different. Very different. This was the first record they had released under their real names, Ant and Dec. Not all that bold, you might think, but it marked a significant gear change.

'They were very bright. They knew exactly what they wanted to do'

In November that year, another single quickly followed – *When I Fall In Love* – which won the boys more acclaim.

That was it. PJ and Duncan had been laid to rest, like a couple of dear departed family members. Gone but not forgotten. And in their place, Ant and Dec's new identities as *themselves* blossomed.

'It's our first single under the name Ant and Dec, so we're quite excited about that,' the lads told the *Newcastle Journal* in the week *Better Watch Out* came out. The single went straight into the charts at Number 10, to the lads' great surprise and delight.

Ant and Dec's rising profile – and their frequent personal appearances on their native Tyneside alongside Geordie mates like footballer Alan Shearer – were providing the region with a welcome promotional boost, and the lads were obviously proud of their roots – and also of their Geordie accents. Down in London, pronounced Geordie accents like theirs were extremely thin on the ground. But that didn't put the boys off. Quite the contrary: 'Nobody's ever told us to get rid of our accents,' Ant insists. 'When we came down to London we had to slow down a bit. Nobody's ever said that to be a hit on TV you've got to speak with a standard British accent. I think it's a good thing. It's like if everyone spoke really straight, it'd get a bit boring.'

Dec was just as excited about their new record release, which he described as part of the duo's 'growing up process' after leaving *Byker Grove*. Reflecting in philosophical mood on the teen soap, Dec had a clear vision of the way ahead. 'The *Byker Grove* chapter is well and truly closed and it's time to move on. People were getting confused, as *Byker Grove* was three years ago, and we felt it was time for a change. We have grown up and learnt a lot. Now we just want to be us. Hopefully that will reflect in the third album, which we're making at the moment and which will be out next February [1997].'

Now they were 'coming of age' as pop stars Ant and Dec, the duo increasingly relished having a creative input into their music. As everyone knows, many boy bands, both then and now, are 'manufactured' by their agents and managers. They rely on singing other artists' songs to launch their own acts, or songwriters step in to offer them numbers to perform. Then it's left to the marketing and promotions teams, the pluggers

'It's our first single under the name Ant and Dec, so we're quite excited about that'

at their record companies, to convince the fans that the new artists have an identity of their own. This was far from the case with Ant and Dec.

They wrote some of their first and all of their second album. 'I think it's something people don't credit us with,' laments Dec. 'We don't, like, shout about it. We just get on, write our songs, and release them when we're happy with them. We go into the studio with the producers and we're not afraid to say that, yeah, we make pop songs – we're a pop band. And we try to make the best pop songs we can, with the hookiest choruses and the best sing-alongs.'

Their album *The Cult of Ant and Dec* was riding high in the charts as the pair took centre stage on the last Saturday night in May in Newcastle's City Hall, sending the screaming crowds wild by performing all their hits including *Shout*, *Let's Get Ready To Rhumble*, *When I Fall in Love* and their latest release *Falling*. The pair looked a pretty picture, with their trendy clothes and pageboy haircuts with centre partings, as they pranced and pirouetted through their neatly choreographed dance routines. Their perfectly co-ordinated bouncy steps became an integral part of their act (even though, looking back nowadays, the boys cringe and laugh at how they used to look).

They even managed to pay homage to the footballing hero Alan Shearer and their beloved Newcastle United by singing a number in the team's famous black and white striped kit.

A journalist at the show loved every minute of it. 'The duo provided 100 per cent home-grown entertainment,' he wrote. 'A fitting way to end their UK tour. Oh, and the audience lapped it up ... If there were ever two lads who deserved the big time, it's these two. Unpretentious, funny, charming, and having a right royal laugh, they held court at the City Hall like Shearer at St James'.

'Just goes to show what a bit of canny Geordie cheek and a couple of winning smiles can do, eh?

Looking back, Dec beams one of his famous cheeky smiles. 'We loved being pop stars. We went everywhere in limos, we were mobbed outside hotels, and we got to go places that we would never have seen otherwise, like Japan and Australia. What teenage boy wouldn't want that?'

After their success in establishing themselves as Ant and Dec, their travelling commitments and TV work made it increasingly difficult for them to be based in the Northeast. So, for the first time, they moved to London and, by 1996, they were sharing a rented flat together in trendy Fulham. They lived together for three years and Dec says that he and Ant shared great times. But there were times when Ant needed his time alone and he'd disappear to his room to play his tapes. Generally, though, the pair would like nothing more than to come home after a hard day's work in the studio, dump their bags and scripts in the hall and slump down in front of the telly with a beer. They might play Striker on the PlayStation or watch one of their favourite videos, like *Only Fools and Horses*. They often used to wind each other up. When one of them had a girlfriend coming round, as a tease, the other one would sneak into the bedroom and drape knickers over the headboard. Often the lads would share a joke and visitors to the flat wouldn't understand what it was about. For years, Dec has been a crazy Morecambe and Wise fan and he never stops repeating their gags, which he knows off by heart. Ant loves to tune into the humour – but not everyone is on their wavelength.

But after a few months' cohabitation Ant discovered Dec's flaw. 'Housework was very low on the agenda,' says Ant. 'Dec was very messy.' Dec's favourite trick was 'clearing up' old newspapers and mags by simply arranging them in a pile – he'd never throw them away. The clutter got worse and worse.' Dec had this incredibly annoying habit of leaving the butter out of the fridge overnight so that it was all soft and squidgy in the morning.'

Ant reckons Dec's most annoying habit was, and still is, that he sometimes doesn't listen to what people say to him. (Dec admits this is true.) Indeed the two lads have quite different outlooks and personalities. For example, Dec reckons Ant is much quieter than he is. 'He's a thinker, but also a great laugh,' says Dec. If you're in the mood to have a silly conversation with someone, then Ant's yer man! But Dec reckons Ant's house habits are no laughing matter. Ant is a 'messy bathroom man', he complains. When they lived together, Ant left toothpaste all over the basin and towels were tossed into the bath tub. Ugh! Dec is quite candid about Ant's most disgusting habit. 'He wees on the toilet seat.' (Ant protests it wasn't his fault. It's just that the toilet seat wouldn't stay up. Now he takes more care with his aim.)

But despite his domestic shortfalls, Dec reckons Ant is a calming influence on balance and cooler under pressure than he is because he always keeps things in perspective.

As all this domestic bliss was going on, Ant and Dec were deciding to 'set up shop' together in another field – professionally. Their flatshare wasn't to prove their only partnership that year, because 1996 also marked a major decision to strengthen their ties even more on the work front. It was a move, in the autumn of '96, that greatly affected their television careers – and, no doubt, their bank balances!

49

On screen, the Geordie duo had developed an easygoing air, as if they make light of their own jobs and careers. It's only telly, after all. But, in view of where they'd come from and where their ambitions lay, what they did next must have seemed pretty daunting and momentous. Their BBC-based *Ant and Dec Show* had earned the pair their first BAFTA Award for Best Kids' Show, which boosted their confidence. Pretty soon, plenty of rival producers were knocking on their doors. To prove they were not just pretty faces, Ant and Dec made a very smart decision that ensured they maximised their earnings while increasing their creative input into their shows. As 1997 loomed, at the ripe old age of 22, they decided it was time they created themselves a little space – and 'street-cred' as businessmen. Together with some partners they set up their own independent production company, and they named it – yes, you guessed – Ant and Dec Productions Ltd. This company gave them the freedom to strike deals anywhere they wished, not just with the BBC.

'We wanted more control of our careers,' explains Ant. 'We had lots of good ideas that we were keen to develop. We thought that if we owned our own company, we could get sacked by the BBC or whoever and still work.

'Famous people have a shelf-life – unless they're like George Michael or Madonna and can keep on reinventing themselves. People can grow tired of you and that could happen to us, too. At least having our own company means we can go on making programmes for other people, even if we aren't in front of the camera ourselves.'

Ant and Dec's decision to set up their own company so early on didn't just mean they craved creative independence. It also proved that they are shrewd business operators. But picture Ant and Dec as company directors and you can forget the stereotyped image of pinstriped suits in the boardroom, reading out minutes from the last meeting and sticking to a formal agenda. Oh, no! Boardroom protocol, when Ant and Dec are in the big leather chairs at the end of the table, takes on a whole new guise.

'We own the company with two partners. It's really funny,' Ant giggles, dropping his guard, the cautious and reserved side for which he is famous. 'We have board meetings and get really bored. We pass notes to one another and make paper airplanes. We're true executives.'

Dec, equally unconcerned with corporate formalities, chips in merrily, 'We chair board meetings, buy scripts, sign cheques. We're not like Chris Evans though. We don't shout!'

Heartened by the successful run of the first series of *The Ant and Dec Show*, the two presenters made their second series even more entertaining. Some of the games in the studio 'pushed the boat out' a little further, with kids in the studio audience being pulled out for a bit of good-natured fun, like the quiz game *Beat the Barber*, in which the young contestants either won a PlayStation or lost their hair.

It was all pretty good-humoured, and the show's researchers made efforts in advance to OK it with everyone involved, including the kids, their parents and schools. But although the kids loved the show some adults did not, and the quiz still drew a mixed postbag from some anxious mums and dads. And the 'suits' at the BBC didn't like that. The complaints forced the publicly accountable corporation executives responsible for the Beeb's good, clean name to have a hurried rethink.

The final outcome was that the BBC decided to re-edit the show, a move that really upset Ant and Dec, who had invested a great deal of time, effort and creative thought in the programme's preparation. Their professional pride was dented and they felt wounded by the decision. But the biggest casualty of the whole unhappy episode, as it turned out, was their relationship with the BBC itself.

The suits' decision made Ant and Dec 'consider their position' at the BBC, who they felt were being unreasonable in taking an edge out of the programme and making it too bland. For once, Ant and Dec showed their teeth. Asked for his reaction to the BBC's decision at the time, Dec pulled no punches: 'Heartbreaking. To make a series and then, after the first couple of shows have gone out, they pull the rest of the series in and re-edit them so they are as tame as they could possibly be. Then say, "Right, let's make a third series," and we're like, "There's no point. We won't be happy. It won't be a show we want to make."

'It was just turning us into normal children's presenters. They think children's telly should be *Blue Peter*, it should be good and wholesome. I don't disagree with that but I think you have to push boundaries. I didn't watch *Blue Peter* when I was a kid. That wasn't how my life was. I could never relate to telly like that, and there are loads of kids who can't. Growing up on a council estate in Newcastle, I never made models of things out of cereal packets. I was climbing trees and playing football.

'The ITC [TV watchdog the Independent Television Commission] have been watching us for years. I imagine them like New York cops all sitting around going, "One slip-up and I'm gonna nail 'em!"'

Ant's nose was equally put out of joint. 'It's Auntie, isn't it?' he added. 'The channel you can put your kids in front of and feel pleased with yourself. We challenged that so that it reflected the playground a bit more. Kids are cooler than people like to think. We've always said that we aren't going to be patronising. The end result shocked people a bit.'

Throughout this time, Ant and Dec were still working hard recording their third album and by the time it was out the pop stars' TV career had taken a new turn. Ant and Dec had defected to Channel 4.

The chance to front a slightly more risqué programme on C4, the livelier and more cutting-edge *Ant and Dec Unzipped*, proved irresistible to the boys, who seemed by now to have had their bellyful of BBC red tape. The Channel 4 deal was reportedly to the tune of £300,000.

This defection was a bold move and a cleverly thought-out strategy, no doubt plotted by both Ant and Dec and their management. But the decision to leave the BBC must have been a hard one for the two boys, despite Auntie's nagging. The duo's anarchic and irreverent style, their fondness for rocking the establishment boat, had nudged them out of the BBC groove and they had to move on.

Switching to Channel 4 in 1997 also signalled to the industry as a whole that the pair were not content to sit back and rest on their laurels. The move made it clear to the outside world that they were determined not to be pigeonholed as BBC stalwarts for the rest of their lives. They had their own personal careers to think of and they were prepared to take their talent to the channel that most appealed to them at that time. And the business wished them good luck.

The change of TV allegiance also involved a masterstroke that was to spark many comparisons in later years with two of the nation's greatest comedy legends, Morecambe and Wise. The Geordie duo hired Eric and Ernie's scriptwriter, Eddie Braben, to write them some material for the new show. 'The scripts he sent us were magical,' acknowledges Ant. 'There was stuff that you could picture Eric and Ernie doing so well. It was slightly intimidating. I didn't think we could pull that off, especially not then. It was still the early days. We were still in a pop band doing these pop videos where the director would be going, "Right, be sultry, be boy band, be pin-up." Then we'd go into the studio and they'd go, "Right. We want you to be a Chinese magician and his assistant."'

Weird!

In addition to *Ant and Dec Unzipped*, Channel 4 invited Ant and Dec to help front their daily morning show *The Big Breakfast* alongside Denise Van Outen and Lily Savage. The end of 1997 also saw Ant and Dec hosting the Smash Hits Pollwinners Party on Channel 4 along with the one-off *Ant and Dec's Geordie Christmas*. Early in 1998 they also stood in for Johnny Vaughan and Denise van Outen for another stint on *The Bigger Breakfast*. Their third album, *The Cult of Ant and Dec*, carried on selling well. And as the two young Geordies juggled the demands of their TV and music careers, their fame and their fan base continued to grow.

But despite the success they'd found at Channel 4, they were soon to enter a round of secret negotiations with another channel, which was to become their new home before long. They knew that ITV was their gateway to a larger, more mainstream audience.

Ahead lay another massive opportunity, a raft of exciting new entertainment shows. *SM:tv Live*, *cd:uk*, *Slap Bang*, *Pop Idol* and a string of one-off spectaculars. These shows, which attracted increasingly large audiences, were to turn Ant and Dec from cult heroes into household names.

The days were already over when they were famous only on Tyneside, when they could pop down to the corner shop in London for a paper without being recognised and mobbed by autograph hunters. Ant and Dec were soon to become highly sought-after mainstream popular entertainers, two of the most wanted faces on British television. Before long they would be able to command magazine front covers, telephone number salaries, the pick of formats they wanted to work with, and primetime audiences running into many millions.

On the pop stardom front, the glamour and glitz of being teen idols was starting to fade. Their schedule, which had taken them on overseas tours, performing their songs over and over again, was becoming a grind. Chasing all over the place, being mobbed by fans and autograph hunters, seemed great fun at the time – but the boys' punishing schedule, globetrotting, performing, conducting interviews, jumping on and off airliners, and the inevitable jet lag, was soon to take its toll.

'We got sick of doing the music,' says Ant. 'Pop life was just so relentless. We were sitting in a taxi one day after recording some stuff for a potential fourth album and I just turned round and said, "I'm not enjoying this any more." And Dec said, "I'm not either. Shall we bother with it any more?" And I said, "No."'

Dec is just as honest. 'We did all the dance routines, TV shows and pop mags, but didn't ever think of ourselves as real musicians. We always knew we were scamming it. I think even our fans knew that.'

The lure of more entertainment television work helped make their minds up – and, as before, they were not afraid to take brave decisions.

They say that, in entertainment television, presenters need their own catchphrase. All the big names in the business have theirs. Rolf Harris has his famous 'Can you tell what it is yet?' For Brucie it's 'Nice to see you, to see you nice', Larry Grayson wanted everyone to 'shut that door' and Cilla loves having a 'lorra lorra laughs' on Blind Date. Ant and Dec soon developed a catchphrase of their own, which they liked to shout out to the viewers at home. Whenever the duo's programme went into a commercial break, they would seemingly chastise any viewer tempted to switch over channels during the adverts. Urging the viewer to stay tuned to the Ant and Dec show, the Geordie twosome would point their fingers straight at the camera and shout,

'You know where it's at!'

Well, their catchphrase worked. And, thanks to an army of hard-working supporters behind the scenes – agents, producers, writers and researchers, as well as executives in the corridors of power – the careers of these two Tyneside tearaways were being magically transformed.

'You know where it's at!'

The ambitious Newcastle teenagers of the 1980s had grown up fast. And they'd proved they had the staying power to be different from so many of their contemporaries. Ant and Dec, and their management, were smart enough to know what constituted staying power. They were wise enough to reinvent themselves when they needed to, and had the bravery to take tough decisions about their future when they needed to. Crucially, they also made many friends and few enemies in the industry.

They kept on track as the 1990s progressed, continuing slowly on their steady upwards climb to becoming the new 'Golden Boys of ITV'.

That label was a tough ticket, and they knew it. Soaking up the pressures of primetime, coping with the stresses of working live in the studio, living up to the expectations of their agents and the network schedulers ... all these burdens combined had, in the past, defeated others, including TV hosts more experienced than themselves.

Ant and Dec also knew that the sometimes fickle and fluctuating world of television could nurture and promote presenters and then spit them out. The newspapers have often been criticised, too, for building someone up and then bringing about their downfall. At times, the pressure of their careers was to weigh heavily on their young shoulders. But they both bore the responsibility well and wore the mantle with pride.

20 Things you Never Knew about Cow Eyes and Santa Claus

Here are some quirky quickies about Ant and Dec that you never knew.

1 Ant's nicknames are Forehead, Smiler and Cow Eyes (well, Dec says he can be mooooody).

2 When Ant turns out for a game of footie with the lads, he likes to play in goal. Dec plays in midfield.

3 The first record Dec ever bought was *Living Doll* by Cliff Richard.

4 Ant rarely gets nervous when interviewing celebrities, but he did get sweaty palms when he had to chat to Blur – because they are his favourite band.

5 TV and pop music have brought Ant fame and fortune. But he'd willingly trade it all in to make his dream come true. 'I would have loved to have been a footballer,' he told *cd:uk* magazine. 'But I was never good enough. If I could click my fingers and swap everything I've got now to play for Newcastle United, I would.'

6 Apart from playing football with Lee from Steps every week, Ant doesn't hang around much with celebrities. Neither does Dec.

7 After a hard day's work in the studio, Ant likes nothing more than to come home and cook for his girlfriend, Lisa (lots more details about the lovely Lisa shortly). He says he finds it relaxing.

8 The worst holiday Dec ever took was when he flew to the Bahamas. The hotel was full of kids who kept dive-bombing in the swimming pool, shouting, 'Watch me, Dec.' Then he got the squits. At the weekend Newcastle were playing Man Utd, but he couldn't find a TV with a satellite dish. He couldn't wait to jet home.

9 Dec is an awful cook. He can manage beans on toast and spaghetti hoops – but that's about his limit.

10 If Dec were ever booked to appear on a celebrity edition of *Stars In Their Eyes*, he'd want to be Paul McCartney because he's a huge Beatles fan.

11 Dec has many hidden talents – one of them is roller blading. 'I'm the master,' says Dec. 'I started when I was 14 and pretty soon I had a black belt in blading and local children were coming to me for lessons.' Dec also gave *cd:uk* magazine his top tips:

- when skating, use both legs and flap your arms

- whatever you do, don't look down

- the most important trick to master is the Bum Flip (that's when you fall on your butt). I usually pad out my pants with socks to make the move more comfy before sliding around on my botty with a fixed smile on my face. The girls go wild for it. Your date'll be circling you for snogs in no time!

12 Dec keeps his awards in his spare bedroom at home (so if you get to visit and stay overnight, you can take a peek).

13 Dec shares his birthday – 25 September – with a host of famous names including Catherine Zeta Jones and her husband, Hollywood heart-throb Michael Douglas, actors Will Smith and Felicity Kendal and model Jodie Kidd.

14 When Dec goes home for Christmas, the Donnelly home is filled with kids – Dec's three brothers and three sisters, plus the 10 grandchildren – and Dec likes to dress up as Santa Claus to give them all a treat.

15 In 2001 teeth-whitening experts Pearl Drops conducted a survey to mark National Kissing Day. The aim was to find out who has the sexiest, most snoggable lips. Miss Hotlips 2001 was *Pearl Harbor* star Kate Beckinsale. Clinching the Mr Hotlips title (by a landslide victory), step forward both Ant and Dec, who claimed 64 per cent of the vote. They beat Tom Cruise (28 per cent) and youth TV presenter Dermot O'Leary.

16 Award-winning actress Helen Mirren idolises Ant and Dec. 'I think they are both geniuses, I really do,' raves Helen, 'and they are so cute. Whenever I am in Britain, I get up early on Saturdays so that I can watch their show in peace and just enjoy what they do. I think my husband is getting a bit jealous.'

17 Ant and Dec were among a range of celebrities who autographed Christmas cards last year before they were auctioned online for charity. Participants included Steps, S Club 7, A1 and the judges from *Pop Idol*. All proceeds went to Woolworth's Kids First, which supports community-based children's projects nationwide.

18 Ant's favourite colour is blue. Dec's is orange.

19 Ant's star sign is Scorpio. Dec is a Libra.

20 One reason why the lads get along so well is that they share similar interests – with one exception. Ant explains, 'Luckily we do have different tastes in women. I always go for brunettes and Dec likes blondes.'

That Tyneside Magic

At first glance, Ant and Dec appear to have moved seamlessly and confidently around the industry, almost ever since they left school and landed plum roles in the TV series *Byker Grove*. But this is not quite the whole truth. For a start, there have been plenty of moments of self-doubt along the way, anxious times when they were both unsure about what the future held in store for them. Later on in their careers, some of their TV shows proved a little disappointing in the ratings at first. However, Ant and Dec were never too big for their boots to take stock and have a rethink if one was required.

This ability to reflect soberly on their own predicament came out in conversation with journalist Jan Moir, who shared an intriguing chat with the two boys about their remarkable success story – and how close they had sometimes sailed to the wind. Jan observed, 'They took careful note of what happened to them during the lean periods – who remained friendly, who never bothered to return their calls – and today they feel that this has stood them in good stead. It has certainly given them humility and they remain nice, decent boys.'

Another reason why we warm to Ant and Dec's charm is that they seem genuinely to enjoy each other's company. They find each other entertaining and amusing and their friendship is infectious.

Their closeness even extends to their everyday conversation. Like all the best double acts who are really in tune with each other and pick up on each other's comedy timing, Ant will often finish Dec's sentences for him, and vice versa. They also travel abroad on holiday together with their girlfriends, and are often out socialising as a foursome.

But the time came when they both, individually, felt the need to invest in a home of their own. And their decision to move apart and stop living together under the same roof definitely had nothing to do with rumours (which they laughed off) that their own relationship was more than 'just friends'!

Dec picks up the story. 'I saw this little development that was up for sale and asked Ant to come along as I'd like his opinion on the houses. So he stayed outside, had a look around. I came out with the estate agent and said, "That's great. I'll take that one please." Ant was standing there and said, "That one over there, is it for sale? Could I have a look?" So he bought it. We looked at each other and went, "Aw no, people are really going to start talking now!" But we're best pals. We've moved away from home and we still haven't that many good, close friends here in London. There's no point in living on the other side of town from each other.'

The luxury homes they ended up buying – smart, three-bedroomed Victorian houses in Chiswick, west London – are situated in the same cul-de-sac, just two doors away from each other.

Domestic comforts are clearly important to the boys, and at first glance these two lovable Geordies appear to be just like any other lads who enjoy a bevvie, a game of footie and a night out with their lassies, both of whom are glamorous girls with showbusiness in their blood.

ANT & DEC Loving Every Second!

Dec's girlfriend is his childhood sweetheart, actress Clare Buckfield. Originally from Elstree, near London, Clare found fame playing Jenny in TV's hit series *2point4 Children*. She first met Dec 10 years ago, when he was on *Byker Grove* and Clare was appearing in the school soap *Grange Hill*.

Ant's love is make-up artist and former singer with teen band Deuce, Lisa Armstrong. They have been dating for the past seven years. Both girls get on famously with Cat Deeley, Ant and Dec's *SM:tv* co-host. But however solid and secure Ant and Dec have become in their loving relationships with Lisa and Clare, neither of the boys has any plans to marry their long-term girlfriends just at the moment. They do admit though, that as they do most things together, they have thought about a double wedding one day. 'We've got no plans but a joint wedding would be funny,' ponders Dec.

Even though all four of them have links to the entertainment business, the romantic stories of how they met reveal that our superstars are ordinary at heart. Their relationships are straightforward and lasting ones, rather than fleeting affairs that might grace the pages of some glossy magazine one day and be history the next. Because Ant and Dec's homes are so close to each other, the two couples spend lots of time at each other's houses.

Dec recently opened his heart to reveal some of his innermost emotions, both about his friendship with his TV partner and his love for his life partner. 'I feel so lucky,' he confessed. 'I hope that everybody in their life would find the friendship that I've got with Ant and the love I've got with Clare. It's more important than money you earn; it's the best thing you can have.'

Dec told *Bliss* magazine he first spotted Clare at Alton Towers theme park in Staffordshire, when he was acting in *Byker Grove* and she was a member of the cast of *Grange Hill*. Clare, a petite blonde, slim and attractive with a big cheeky grin, has that 'girl-next-door' look about her – and she immediately caught Dec's eye.

'I fancied her so I tried to blag an introduction. I kept trying to get into her group but each time I did, she turned and walked away.'

A whole year passed before Dec saw Clare again. He asked her out for a drink at a local pub and waited 45 minutes before she finally arrived. 'Suddenly there she was. It was the middle of November. We went out into the beer garden and there was ice everywhere. She said she was freezing so I pulled her in under my jacket … and we kissed. It was such a different feeling to anything I'd ever felt before. My belly was going mad and my head was a bit dizzy.'

At first, when Declan confided in his friend Ant and told him about the relationship, Ant enjoyed ribbing him about it. But soon, Ant had reasons of his own to take such feelings seriously. 'Then I met Lisa,' recalled Ant, smitten in an instant. Lisa is a sophisticated and elegant brunette with a sexy, smouldering smile that set Ant on fire! 'The only person who knew I liked her was Dec. It was a bit of an insecurity thing because I wasn't sure she liked me. Once we started seeing each other though, we'd speak on the phone every other day, then every night, then a few times a day, and then most of the day. We were just talking rubbish but it didn't matter because we were talking to each other.'

Neither Ant nor Dec is in any particular hurry to get married, and they both feel that such developments will take their course naturally when the time is right. When Dec goes home to Newcastle and sees his old schoolfriends, many of whom are already married with children, he finds that slightly scary. While his friends seem to have taken such responsibilities in their stride, Dec freely admits he doesn't yet feel quite ready to take on the burdens of parenthood, although he does want kids of his own – and he wants four of five of them!

'I'm going to be the coolest dad in the world,' he's told fans. 'I'm really looking forward to it.'

Dec says, when he's married, he would love to have one child by the time he's 30. 'But the time has to be right and I don't want any of these divorces,' he says.

One thing's for certain, of course. When Ant and Dec do finally tie the knot with their respective girlfriends and announce that they are getting married, it will surely break the hearts of millions of their adoring girl fans. No one would be surprised if there were an outbreak of weeping and wailing on the streets of Newcastle when news of the weddings breaks – in pretty much the same way that Beatle fans mourned Paul McCartney's announcement that he was getting married and giving up his title as Britain's most eligible bachelor.

'I'm going to be the coolest dad in the world,' he's told fans. 'I'm really looking forward to it.'

63

As for the enduring friendship between the two lads themselves, Dec has a little theory about why he and Ant have stayed such close mates over the years. 'We had our ups and downs. We had to grow up quick, much of it has been insecure and sporadic. What Ant and I crave is a little consistency. That is why we have been constants in each other's lives and have had long-term relationships with our girlfriends.'

Canny, that.

While Ant and Dec's long-term partnerships with their girlfriends were flourishing and their friendship with each other grew stronger, another, perhaps even more important long-term relationship was, by contrast, coming to an end. Dave Holly, their Newcastle-based manager, who had so skilfully represented and advised them for many years, ceased to be their main agent in 1998, when Ant and Dec moved to James Grant Management in London.

The career move was clearly a significant step for the two presenters. By signing with the new agency, which represents some of the biggest names in the business, they were tapping into a wealth of experience and kudos offered by the high profile and prestigious firm. The list of celebrities Ant and Dec can now count as fellow clients at their agency includes household names such as Phillip Schofield, Andi Peters, Anthea Turner, Anna Walker and the lovely Caron Keating, daughter of everyone's favourite, Gloria Hunniford.

Psychologically, the change of agent came at a crucial time for the presenters, who were gearing up for a brand new assault on our TV screens. Within months ITV unleashed a new vehicle for Ant and Dec, boldly presenting them as the 'cheeky chappy' front men for a brand new Saturday morning kids' show. After working hard to prepare a string of hilarious new comedy sketches, jokes and games for the programme, Ant and Dec had their fingers and toes tightly crossed in the hope that their show would prove a big hit with the public and make their audience laugh.

But if you had frozen Ant and Dec in that moment, in the summer of 1998, and told them they'd be fronting the new series for the next *three and a half years*, they'd no doubt have shaken their heads in total disbelief.

Saturday Morning Madness

Pop stardom had given way to TV stardom in 1998 as Ant and Dec put their singing careers behind them and concentrated on developing their small-screen personas on ITV.

Top-secret plans were afoot to relaunch Ant and Dec as the independent network's major new stars of children's TV. And after a lengthy 'gestation period', during which plans and ideas were drawn up for the exciting new series, *SM:tv Live* finally arrived on air in August 1998.

!@?*!

Ant and Dec were thrilled and flattered that they had reached a stage in their careers at which both the BBC and ITV were battling hard for their attentions. When *SM:tv Live* launched on Saturday 29 August 1998, it marked the end of twelve months' secret planning. Ant and Dec had had to keep their ideas strictly under wraps because the BBC would have been furious if they had found out that the duo were plotting to go head-to-head with the Beeb's rival *Live and Kicking*.

But clever Ant and Dec knew precisely what they were doing by sparking a furious ratings battle for Saturday morning viewers – a battle they were to win hands down.

What no one knew then was that *SM:tv Live* was to become the first ITV Saturday morning programme to overtake the BBC in the ratings for 30 years. Ant and Dec so comprehensively beat the competition, the BBC ran up the white flag.

!@?*!

In 2001 *The Saturday Show* on BBC1 pulled in an audience of around 800,000 viewers, compared with the 2.5 million who watched *SM:tv Live*. When the Geordie duo helped dream up the format for *SM:tv Live*, they agreed that the magic extra ingredient they needed to add was a glamorous female presenter in between them to make up a trio.

When the news got out that the hunt was on for someone to fill that role, hundreds of showreel tapes were sent in by female presenters hoping to be shortlisted for an audition. Among them was a fresh-faced gorgeous young presenter who was working for the satellite music channel MTV, named Cat Deeley.

The lads knew immediately that Cat was the one for them – because as soon as she arrived she started taking the mickey out of them both mercilessly.

Crafty Cat had made a few enquiries about the boys, and had heard about an embarrassing story in a Chinese restaurant. Both Ant and Dec had been so drunk, reportedly, that they had fallen off their chairs – and Dec had exchanged a few harsh words with one guy there.

*I*n her interview, Cat pretended that she was the girlfriend of that guy – and Ant and Dec, who couldn't remember a thing about the meal, were forced to apologise to her. 'I seem to remember you gave my boyfriend a bit of a mouthful,' she told them, making it up as she went along.

Three hours later, Cat couldn't keep up her pretence any longer. She admitted that she had been sneakily winding them up – and she promptly got the job!

Cat was born in Sutton Coldfield, Birmingham on 26 October 1976, making her nearly a year younger than the boys. She went to Dartmouth High School, then attended Bishop Vesey school. She was a bit of a brainbox, achieving nine grade As at GCSE and four A levels.

Her early career ambitions hovered somewhere between being a *Blue Peter* presenter and Julie Andrews in *The Sound of Music*. Then she went through a phase of thinking she wanted to be a doctor or a lawyer. And when she wasn't swotting up for her exams, Cat was pretty active both in and out of school. She appeared in lots of her school plays – providing the perfect training ground for her later starring role in *Chums*.

Cat was in the Brownies and the Guides, and she played piano and the clarinet, talents which came in useful in the school orchestra. Outdoors, hockey was her favourite sport. These days, Cat has remained a keep-fit enthusiast and she's got a mean right hook! She trains at a gym in north London that's full of professional boxers with smashed-out teeth, preparing for fights. 'My trainer, Roy, actually tells people that I can punch quite hard for a girl,' says Cat with a laugh.

When she was just 14, Cat's glamorous looks won her a modelling competition (shame on Ant and Dec for nicknaming her 'Cat the Dog' on the show). She came first in a BBC *Clothes Show* competition, and her catwalk success led to the TV work – in 1998 she joined MTV as a video jock.

Despite their earlier links with the BBC, as *SM:tv Live* found its feet the Geordie presenters weren't afraid to take the occasional side-swipe at the corporation. In one show Cat tried to read a link several times in the studio – but fluffed her line. Sitting between the boys on the sofa as usual, she pretended to be desperately upset, leapt up, stamped her feet in protest and stormed off the set with an impetuous flounce. As she strode off to the wings, exit stage right, she shouted back angrily at Ant & Dec, 'I'm going to be where I can be alone and not bothered.'

The audience thought she was on her way to her dressing room. But Ant shouted back, pointing the other way. Redirecting Cat to exit stage left, he yelled, 'The BBC's that way!'

The 'in-joke' went down well with the ITV crew!

When the show went out live on Saturday morning all three presenters gave the impression that they were working off the cuff. But the truth is that hours of painstaking preparations are made, involving everyone on the production team. Not just the presenters, but the writers, directors, camera crew and researchers run through the show several times, to ensure it goes with a swing when the celebrity guests finally arrive.

One of Dec's favourite sections in the show is Postbag, to which viewers of all ages send in quirky odds and ends. During the summer months, when fans go abroad on their holidays, they often come across foreign confectionery with rude names. They send in the wrappers to Ant and Dec in the studio, who read them out live on air. There was the chocolate bar named Fart, for example. But the material that viewers sent in went through 'a bit of a dark phase' according to the presenters. One viewer sent in a wart, another posted the boys

Ant with Kylie Minogue

some dog sick, and there was an envelope containing toenail clippings from an old people's home. The final straw came when one woman had her cat neutered and she sent in its privates. That was when the team decided it was time to lighten things up a bit.

And talking of keeping things light and airy, there was one golden moment Ant, Dec and Cat will never forget. They had asked the kids to write in with stories about all the embarrassing things their dads got up to at home. One youngster contacted the show to reveal that his father liked to secretly fart in the family biscuit tin, close the lid quickly – and then offer the tin around to the boy's friends. Fits of hysterical giggles struck everyone in the studio – especially Ant and Dec, who kept imagining the man with his bum over the tin!

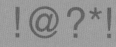

And still on the subject of bums, Dec's would get its fair amount of attention during the show – from the studio audience. Youngsters in the studio loved to put Dec off his stride during the show. While he was trying to concentrate on his lines, girls would often make a lunge for his bum. 'The

'It was nice – but weird'

!@?*!

worst thing is when you're trying to concentrate on your lines and your buttocks are being grabbed,' Dec explained. 'They grab handfuls of my buttocks. The worst was somebody kind of poking a finger in between!'

There can sometimes be a flip-side to being famous as a kids' TV presenter. Cat was in the supermarket buying her groceries one day when three 14 year-old girls walked up and, standing in the aisle, gave an impromptu performance of the Postbag song and dance. Cat commented later, 'It was nice – but weird.'

Ant and Dec's willingness to experiment by spoofing fellow stars have also endeared them to fans of all generations. A fine example of the duo's zany sense of humour came when Ant, Dec and Cat donned moth-eaten, long curly wigs in a tongue-in-cheek St Patrick's Day tribute to the family band The Corrs. Mimicking the thick Irish accents of the real Corrs singers, Ant, Dec and Cat pouted sexily at the camera and in husky voices struck up a chorus of the word 'beautiful' – pronounced 'bee-yood-iful'.

Ant and Dec with Dame Dolly, played by actor Peter Thorne

!@?*!

'We're bee-yood-iful. We're so bee-yood-iful. Because we're the bee-yood-ifull Corrs. Yes, we're bee-yood-iful,' they kept repeating. It sounded hilarious.

On another show Ant slicked back his hair, slipped on a pair of shades and a leather jacket and took off U2 frontman Bono. Then Dec dressed as an Irish dancer, Michael Flatley-style, and later transformed himself into a leprechaun.

The presenters always play a leading part in creating and developing the comedy element in the ideas and games on the show, from early script development through to the ad libs that make the final programme such fun. Ant and Dec's comedy talent – and the way they bounce ideas off each other – are part of what makes them a special, multi-award-winning double act.

Their executive producer Conor McAnally has guided them for many years and has a clear overview of both the style and the content of Ant and Dec's programmes and the two presenters' behaviour in front of camera. Reminiscing to the *Sunday Express* about the success of *SM:tv Live*, Conor illustrated the benefit of his many years of experience. 'It could be argued

Panto at the Sunderland Empire in 1998. Cast as Snow White was Dec's girlfriend Clare Buckfield.

that the children who come on the show don't always get the kindest reception. We've been criticised for not being nicer to the kids. But the crucial thing is not to be patronising. If we run a game where the child gambles something and he loses, he gets nothing. As well as teaching them a valuable life lesson, there's also a big element of humour. When a kid loses, it's very funny.'

A fine example of this occurred in the Challenge Ant section of the show, in which a young contestant risked losing everything he had won during the quiz if Ant managed to score more correct answers. Often the youngster went home empty handed – to Ant's huge delight. 'Frankly, it's great when the kid loses everything,' concluded McAnally. 'People sit there at home watching it with a splitting hangover and think, "Yeah, serves you right, you smart little..."'

Dec has his own distinctive views on the matter. 'We don't play down to the kids. When we were kids, we hated being patronised by presenters. We decided we weren't going to talk down to them [the kids]. If they come on the phone and get a wrong answer for Wonkey Donkey, we'll shout at them and tell them they're stupid. They love it. They don't get upset. People

'Frankly, it's great when the kid loses everything'

71

say we're too cruel to the kids, but the kids love it. They give us back as good as we give them. We try not to be like their mums and dads, responsible adults. We try to be like their cheeky older brothers and take the mickey.'

Ant agrees. 'Our emphasis is on energy, fun and this sense of non-patronising TV,' he emphasises.

On one memorable occasion, a youngster selected to go for the 'Killer Question' and end the quiz round with a 'sudden death play-off'. Ant won, and the boy looked downhearted – until Ant decided to celebrate his victory. Ant leapt up from his chair, grabbed the boy out of his seat, threw him on to his shoulders and whirled him round, as if dancing a jig. The boy, who wasn't much older than six or seven, had no alternative but to share the funny moment with the rest of the studio audience. The stunt won a big laugh, even if it was at the boy's expense.

Celebrity cameos flowed thick and fast on *SM:tv Live*. One Saturday Matthew Kelly from ITV's *Stars In Their Eyes* popped into the studio. Of course, he couldn't resist asking Ant and Dec who they'd like to become on his own wannabe show. Paul McCartney, Dec confessed. Ant's choice was Damon from Blur.

Who knows? Maybe the lads' big chance will come the next time Matthew hosts a celebrity version of his show.

Other stars who've appeared on the show include Emma Bunton and Kylie Minogue, who dressed up in a knee-length skirt, black boots and specs to play a crusty schoolmarm.

Another amazing success was Ant and Dec's spoof serial *Chums*, set in a Newcastle tower block. The popular sketch, which formed a weekly part of *SM:tv Live*'s schedule, was their pastiche of the hit American TV series *Friends*. On one occasion the Geordie version proved a bigger success: a Christmas special of *Chums* attracted 3.5 million viewers, more than *Friends* itself!

Ant and Dec seem to have perfected their image – an easy-going manner, a 'bloke-in-the-pub' charm and a laid-back style.

In the hurly-burly of live broadcasts, when errors and mistakes on the studio floor during a broadcast can often add humour to a show, Ant and Dec's professionalism is unrivalled. Other, less nimble presenters are easily flummoxed by an unforeseen turn of events. But Ant and Dec's ability to react smartly and at speed, in a pressurised situation, frequently adds value to their performance when the camera's red light is on.

These days the vast majority of TV is pre-recorded. Live broadcasts, such as *SM:tv*, are very much the exception to the rule. Surviving the mayhem of live shows means the presenter has also to rely heavily on the professionalism of the producer, director and crew – as Ant and Dec would be the first to acknowledge.

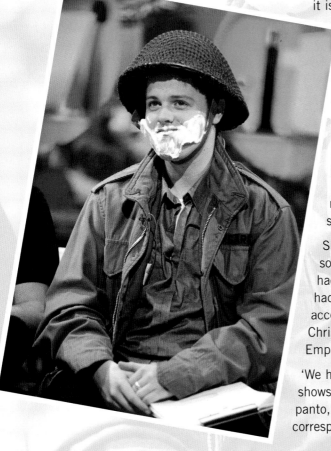

But, at the end of the day, in the eyes of the viewer at home, it is the neck of the presenter 'front of camera' that is on the line when the show goes disastrously wrong. And that's why, when the sound system crashes or the furniture on set falls down, you can always see the terror in the presenter's eyes!

Despite the early success of *SM:tv Live*, the boys had not lost their appetite for other projects – and boosted by the knowledge that they were now much in demand, they decided to spread their wings.

Surprisingly perhaps, one of their first sorties was on to the panto circuit. They had been offered panto roles for years but had always tactfully declined. In 1998 they accepted an invitation to appear, and the Christmas audiences at the Sunderland Empire loved it.

'We have done little bits before in Christmas shows for charity but this is our first real panto,' Dec excitedly explained to local correspondent David Whetstone in the May

SM:tv Live Schedule

Ant and Dec stuck to a hectic schedule for three and a half years as they prepared each week for *SM:tv's* live broadcast. Here's an idea of their weekly timetable running up to the show:

Thursday – two days before the show:

The writers on the programme have finished a draft of the script, which the presenters now run through. As they do so with the producer, everyone irons out any creases that might occur to them, and Ant, Dec and Cat come up with fresh ideas that continue developing right up until the red light flickers on top of the cameras on Saturday morning, still 48 hours away.

Friday – the day before the show:

Guests and presenters turn up at the London Studios on the capital's South Bank for full rehearsals. There is much laughter and larking about, but underneath it all the team know that they have to get it right when they go live to the nation.

In the evening, just as town is livening up, Cat, Ant and Dec head off home to bed as they have to be up incredibly early the next morning. It's a drag not to be allowed out with all their friends on a Friday night, but the trio are TV professionals first and foremost, and they know that if they party into the small hours before the show, the programme will suffer.

Saturday – Just after 5am:

Ant and Dec's alarm clocks go offand they stumble, groggy and grumpy, from their beds. Outside their Chiswick homes in south-west London, a studio car is waiting to collect them and speed them to the studio on London's South Bank. Just up river, on the banks of the Thames, are the sights that millions of tourists a year cross the world to see: the Houses of Parliament, Big Ben and the Millennium Wheel. But Ant and Dec are too bleary-eyed at this time of the morning to notice.

!@?*!

!@?*!

5.30am: Apart from mumbling 'Mornin'' they haven't spoken to each other since they left home. Ant and Dec are so tired and grumpy, they barely speak to each other. 'Ant and I always arrived in a strop,' admits Dec sheepishly. Now they reach the studio looking forward to their breakfast.

6am: Bacon butties and piping hot coffee are on the menu as the presenters link up with co-star Cat in the breakfast bar. Then it's into make-up before rehearsals in the studio, which start punctually.

7am: Time for a run-through of the script, which still needs fine tuning. The director calls the shots from the gallery, the control box that gives the cameramen on the floor their instructions during the show.

8am: Ant and Dec's celebrity guests start arriving at the studios. The show's two hosts have already been up for three hours.

9.25am: The show goes live on air. During breaks for cartoons, when viewers at home cannot see what is going on in the studio, all hell breaks loose. Stars sprint in and out and the crew race around, keeping up with the split-second timing demanded by the producer and director.

11.30am: In an adjacent section of the studio a fresh audience is brought in for the second section of Ant and Dec's show, *cd:uk*. The studio audience watching and participating in *SM:tv Live* is slightly younger than the *cd:uk* crowd, who are generally aged 18 and over, and who all dance and sway when the music gets going.

12.30pm: At last the show is off the air. It's been an exhausting day. The lads have been at work for nearly seven hours – the same length of working day turned in by most office workers – but it's still only lunchtime. Ant and Dec will head for the bar after the show, or else dash off up to Newcastle to be with their families or to watch the Magpies play at home. Once, Ant and Dec asked British Airways to delay a flight for them so they could make the kick-off... but the airline refused.

Now the BBC decided to act. They courted Ant and Dec once again and offered them their own game show, *Friends Like These*. What's more, the slot was to be during primetime on Saturday night. Ant and Dec couldn't resist the challenge. They decided to return to the fold and give their old Auntie another hug.

The BBC1 Saturday night series, which came on air in February 2000, marked Ant and Dec's first major step into primetime TV. Producers advertised for the show, saying they were looking for suitable contestants in the 18 to 30 age bracket who would like to take part.

The new show was all about testing friendships, pitting a handful of boys against a group of girls as they fought it out to win the big prize at the end of the show. Its format, through various quizzes and challenges, tested the skills and general knowledge of the two rival teams. With luxury holiday prizes on offer, the closing stages of each episode were nail-biting affairs, with Ant and Dec joining in the fun too. The friendships between the contestants were tested to the limit. It was a calculated risk by the BBC, and it paid off. The programme proved an instant hit and drew seven million viewers.

Ant explained the format. 'It's all about putting trust in your mates. You really have to know your team-mates well to succeed.'

And Dec reckoned, 'Shows like this don't come along every five minutes. We were keen to do it as it's such a great format. *Friends Like These* is the most fun we've had with five girls and five boys with our clothes on for a long time!'

Ant and Dec were both already long in the tooth enough not to put all their eggs in one basket. And they very wisely continued plugging away with *SM:tv Live* over on ITV. *SM:tv*'s popularity steadily continued growing each week and soon it had become a cult show attracting the biggest stars and the hottest bands. The series had become popular with all generations.

Before long, Ant, Dec and Cat were heading towards a major milestone – they would soon clock up an amazing 100 shows, and a special anniversary edition was planned. The celebrities turned out in force for the spectacular, which aired on Saturday 22 July 2000 and happened to coincide with the

Queen Mum's 100th birthday celebrations. Ant, Dec and Cat were joined by a star-studded cast, including Victoria Beckham, Mel C, Steps, Louise and various *Coronation Street* stars. Dec says he couldn't believe his eyes when so many stars turned out for the show.

The rewards for working so hard on a show don't come better than winning awards – and Ant and Dec have won plenty. In March 2001, *SM:tv Live* scooped the children's entertainment category of the Royal Television Society Awards, a crowning tribute to the presenters and their hard-working team – of which everyone on the show was proud.

!@?*!

And talking of eyes, as part of the episode, Ant pretended he was blind so the guests on the show recorded a spoof charity single for him called *Ant Aid*, to raise funds so that Ant could have an operation on his eyes.

Finally the time came, after three and a half years, for Ant and Dec to bow out of the show. *SM:tv* was to continue – but without them as hosts. Their last show was on Saturday 1 December 2001.

It was a huge disappointment for the crew and production team on the programme – and, of course, for Cat Deeley, whom ITV chiefs invited to stay on. But the unstoppable Geordie duo had decided it was time to move on.

!@?*!

The *News of the World* reported in October that Ant and Dec were devastated to be leaving. But the pair were also excited to be tackling fresh challenges. An 'insider' told the paper,

'There have been stories about them quitting, but they've been completely wrong. ITV landed a great formula with them and Cat [on *SM:tv Live*], but now they want to move on. The boys are gutted they're leaving but they can't do Saturday morning kids' programmes for ever. Mind you, they love the show so much, they may go back.

'The replacements who have made the shortlist so far are Brian Dowling from *Big Brother*, Channel 4's Dermot O'Leary, ex-Boyzone singer Stephen Gately and ex-Five man Ritchie Neville. The last two have been guest presenters, so they have a very good chance.

'Then you've got Dermot who's a natural and would be a very strong contender. But with Brian, they've got an ace card. His popularity would lead telly bosses to hope that the ratings wouldn't fall too much after Ant and Dec left.'

In fact, when the time did finally come for new presenters to step into Ant and Dec's shoes, it was *Hollyoaks* actor James Redmond who took their place at Cat's side. Even though she looked a little lonely without her two Geordie chums at first, Cat soon grew into the main anchor.

*M*s Deeley herself, only days earlier, had managed to spectacularly upstage Ant and Dec elsewhere. The previous Sunday, all three of them had been nominated for a prestigious BAFTA award – but it was Cat who pipped the two boys to the post for the coveted Best Presenter Award.

Her performance on *SM:tv* was rewarded by the honour from the British Academy of Children's Film and Television Awards – and adulation and congratulations from not only Ant and Dec but from many colleagues in the business too.

The last show presented by the threesome was a real tear-jerker, an emotionally supercharged three-hour live show.

'I know everyone says their show is just like one big happy family,' Ant told Heat *magazine, 'but after three-and-a-half years it is like a family. We even play football with two of our producers.'*

The final episode opened with a big musical item. Hardly an inch of the studio could be seen as crowds of celebrities filled the floor for their place at the *SM:tv* Leaving Ball.

Frank Skinner was there, along with David Baddiel, Denise Van Outen, Samantha Mumba, Blue, Carol Vorderman, Hear'Say, Jonathan Wilkes, Robbie Williams, Mark Lamarr and Mariah Carey. A host of other stars sent messages of good luck, with Paul McCartney, David Beckham and U2 leading the recorded tributes. The Corrs sent the lads a signed picture and Victoria Beckham sent a postcard from her holidays with a drawing of her boobs on it. Lisa from Steps sent a card, and as Dec opened the postbag, he admitted, 'It's really hard today. We're going to miss this place so much.'

It was then – 20 minutes into the show – that viewers realised for the first time that the presenters were in floods of tears. Dec's chin was wobbling and Ant could hardly speak.

During another skit titled 'The Secret of my Success', in which Dec would try each week to promote his spoof autobiography, there was a pretend flashback to the set of *Byker Grove*.

In a hilarious send-up of the BBC's hit teen drama, all Ant and Dec's celebrity guests played Geordie teenagers, dressing

!@?*!

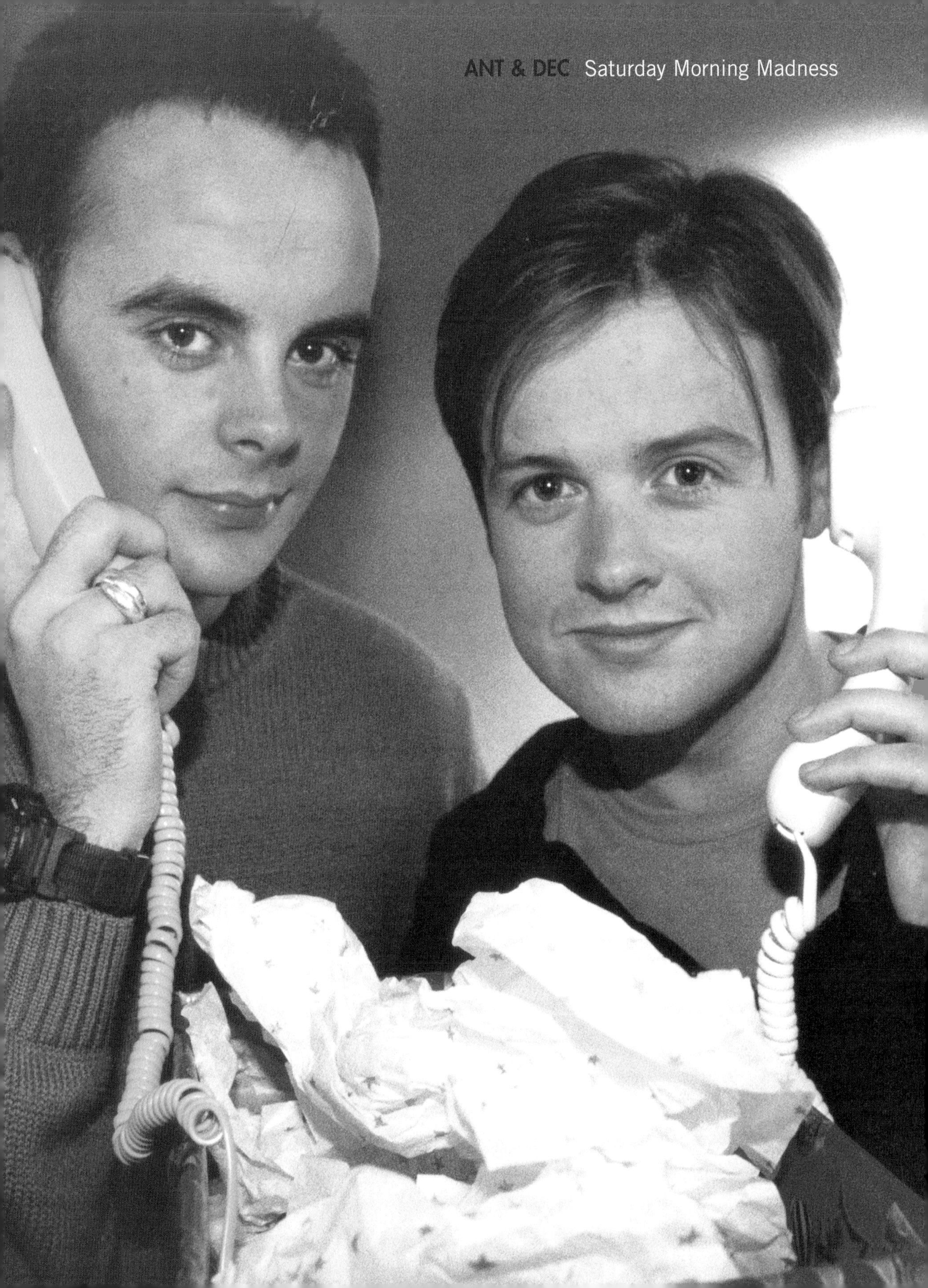

up in bushy wigs and mimicking the Tyneside accent – with varying degrees of success. When another guest, actress Amanda Holden, tried out her appallingly unconvincing Geordie accent, Ant quipped, 'I didn't know she was from Wales – via Scotland, I think.'

Next came the penalty shoot-out competition 'Eat My Goal'. Celebrity contestants like Robbie Williams, Peter Beardsley and David Baddiel all wore Newcastle United shirts as they stepped up to try and beat the goalie - who was Ant.

At the end of the sketch, Robbie Williams surprised the crowd – and the producers – by offering his very own impromptu comedy turn. In an unrehearsed moment of exhibitionism, he dropped his football shorts and bared his backside to camera.

More tributes flooded in from manager Bobby Robson and Alan Shearer at Newcastle. Bobby generously told the lads, 'I know you're both massive Newcastle United supporters. It's why we play so well.'

I t soon became obvious that the producers had rehearsed most sections of the farewell show in advance – for once *without* letting Ant or Dec in on the secret of what had been planned. Coming back to the studio after the commercial break, suddenly the four distinctive notes of the most famous musical intro in British TV rang out in the studio – the theme music to *This is Your Life* ...

Ant and Dec froze in their seats for a moment, then shouted out, 'Oh, no ...' And it looked as if they really thought that Michael Aspel was about to walk on clutching a big red book.

In fact, a man looking nothing like Aspel walked on with a big red book – but it was Frank Skinner, pretending to be Aspel, who appeared. He went on to host a wicked spoof of *This is Your Life*, to the delight of everyone watching.

Asked by Frank what had been so great about fronting the show for so long, Dec replied, 'It's three hours of live TV – just messing about really.'

Ant did let his guard down and own up to one moment that both of them particularly enjoyed – the day their rivals at the BBC announced they were scrapping *Live And Kicking*. Ant confessed, 'We have been quite diplomatic in the past, but I was absolutely over the moon!'

In the final episode of *Chums*, Cat Deeley, as 'Rachel', ended up marrying Dec in a hugely romantic white wedding

'We have been quite diplomatic in the past, but I was absolutely over the moon!'

ceremony, complete with confetti, Mariah Carey as her maid of honour, and Frank Skinner as the priest officiating at the ceremony. Frank, of course, played the cleric as a complete loony, who loved to strip off his robes whenever he got the chance. The climax to the last episode was Dec's long, smoochy kiss, which he planted direct on Cat's lips. Her eyes were full of tears, as the cameramen's close-up pictures revealed to millions of viewers at home. In the final leg of the programme, on *cd:uk*, a host of star turns lined up again to wish the Geordie duo farewell. Kylie Minogue, whom Ant and Dec both admire – and fancy like mad – sent them a video greeting and blew them a sexy kiss. 'Kylie, you do not want to know what the boys are going to do with that video later!', was Cat's knowing response.

Dec asked to see again one of his all-time favourite performances out of 1,990 songs performed on *cd:uk* over the previous three and a half years – REM singing their hit *Losing My Religion*.

And as Dec tearfully told viewers that the show was to be their very last, Ant had to grab his partner to give him a steadying hug. 'This is our last show. We'll be watching next week's show from our beds,' whispered Dec in a wobbly voice.

Ant, snaking his arm round Dec's shoulder, added quickly, 'Hold it together, son. Hold it together.'

Finally, as the closing credits rolled, Ant, Dec and Cat were all in floods of tears, weeping openly as they waved goodbye to the viewers at home and the studio audience. Dec blubbed like a baby, sticking his tongue out to try and stop himself crying, while Ant bit his quivering lip to try to cover up and Cat wiped tears from her eyes.

The next day, the newspapers were full of headlines and pictures marking their tearful departure. Two and a half million viewers had tuned in to see Ant and Dec bid their farewells. That was heartening enough – but also pleasing was the fact that *SM:tv Live* had beaten its BBC rival by a humiliating ratio of three to one. *The Saturday Show*, hosted by Dani Behr, had only managed to attract 800,000.

That said it all.

SM:tv Live Farewell Tributes

The stars turned out in force to bid their fond farewells to Ant and Dec on their last *SM:tv Live*. The two presenters had been kept in the dark about the contents of the show – so each message was a complete surprise. And the flood of messages posted in, recorded on film and delivered in person left Ant and Dec looking shell-shocked and stunned, and finally reduced both Geordie boys to floods of tears. It had been an emotional week for everyone in the music and entertainment business, because the death had just been announced of Beatle George Harrison.

But on a happier note, here are a few of the celebrity tributes that were sent in from around the world:

Sir Paul McCartney

Ant and Dec, you're great. I love ya and I can't wait to see you back again.

Kylie Minogue

Ant, Dec, what can I say? You two are absolutely amazing. I think I bore people silly all over the place telling them how wonderful I think you are. Well done, congratulations and I hope to see you very, very soon.

Sting

I'd just like to say to Ant and Dec, you should come back home to Newcastle and get some proper jobs.

Emma Bunton (Baby Spice)

I've always liked you so give us a call sometime.

David Beckham

I have really enjoyed the last three and a half years. Good luck in the future.

Frank Skinner

Ant and Dec, you are just so fantastic. We love you.

Bobby Robson (Newcastle Utd manager)

Hi, Ant and Dec. I know you're both massive Newcastle United supporters. It's why we play so well. And I know you're going to leave Saturday morning television. I used to watch it. Hey, you're not too bad, quite funny, quite clever. You have done very well and I wish you every success in your lives ahead. I believe you are, as they say, moving forward. Good luck in what you do and keep coming to Newcastle United.

Alan Shearer (Newcastle and former England captain)

I've seen them a few times at the ground and more often than not they get mistaken for the mascots.

Victoria Beckham (Posh Spice)

She sent in a joke postcard from her holiday. It was a large white card on the back of which Posh had etched a small drawing and added doodles around her good luck message. One of the drawings she scribbled as a joke was an outline of her boobs!

Bono, lead singer of U2

You are one of the greatest couples of our time.

There were other recorded tributes from bands including Westlife, and mountains of cards and letters from the stars, including a special message from Steps.

The Corrs, one of Ant and Dec's favourite bands, also sent in a signed, framed picture for them. It was 'bee-yood-ifull'!

'**One is a great admirer of Phil Collins...**'

While Ant and Dec's popularity on *SM:tv Live* had been soaring, ITV executives were determined to cement their relationship with the boys with longer-term contracts. Meanwhile, Ant and Dec's negotiations with the BBC over a possible further series of *Friends Like These* broke down, and ITV stepped in with a lucrative two-year deal.

It sounded like the network couldn't resist gloating. 'We are delighted to be working with Ant and Dec,' said a spokesman. 'They are enormously talented.'

That Christmas, ITV gave their two young stars their own New Year's Day special, *Ant and Dec's Secret Camera Show*. The teatime show featured a series of madcap out-takes and camera clips from all over the world comprising spoofs, practical jokes and some of the most outrageous stunts on TV. For the *Candid Camera*-style show the pair also hit the streets to shoot some of their own stunts. They visited the British Museum to ask ordinary members of the public to stand in as instantly self-appointed and opinionated art experts. That was a hoot!

There were also some 'naughty bits', like one light-hearted scene in which a Belgian waitress appeared to squeeze milk from her breast (which drew a few complaints!). And in another sketch, restaurant-goers were shocked to discover that they were being served by 'cheeky' bare-bottomed waiters.

The Independent Television Commission mentioned 'partly masked nudity' as the cause for offence taken by viewers, one million of whom were under the age of 15, it was estimated.

The broadcaster behind the ITV show argued that the brief nudity was no more than ordinary holidaymakers might see on the beach. But the watchdog upheld the complaints. This wasn't the beach. This eyeful was on TV at five o'clock.

While the silly behind-the-scenes row got ready to rumble, the long and short of it was that Ant and Dec were simply having a spot of fun, getting out and about, being 'at large' rather than stuck in front of a camera in the studio.

'Oh God! I go
through
little periods
of being so
excited and
then
tremendously
scared at the
same time.
But it's a
fantastic
opportunity
for Dec and
I, and it's
something
we've always
wanted to
do.'

In May 2001, Ant and Dec took on a new live show, timed to sit slap-bang in the middle of the primetime schedules on Saturday night. Its title: *Slap Bang*.

The prospect of fronting their own show again, this time during peak viewing time on a Saturday night, certainly fired the lads up and got the adrenaline going, as Ant admitted in an interview with their fans' magazine *cd:uk* during the run-up to the series' launch. 'Oh God! I go through little periods of being so excited and then tremendously scared at the same time. But it's a fantastic opportunity for Dec and I, and it's something we've always wanted to do. But there's also a lot of responsibility on our shoulders.'

Before the series was over, however, fierce competition arrived in the BBC's schedule, in the form of someone who had long been a firm favourite with the viewers. The press made much of a supposed ratings 'duel' between Ant and Dec and the presenter who was to steal some of their audience – Ulrika Jonsson. Ulrika, back on TV screens after taking time out to raise a family, hosted *Dog Eat Dog*, a knock-out entertainment show in which contestants battle to win £10,000.

In the end, the ones who were knocked out were Ant and Dec – after ITV dropped *Slap Bang* from their schedules. Luckily, to make up for their loss, a major treat lay in store...

To say they were nervous is a wild understatement. This was, after all, the very first time in their lives that Ant and Dec, two likely lads from Newcastle's working-class council estates, had met royalty. Their world exclusive interview with Prince Charles was to make an indelible impression on them.

It had been planned to highlight the 25th anniversary of the Prince's Trust charity for young people. And for their epic royal encounter, the boys travelled down to the Prince's sumptuous Highgrove home, set in the lush green acres of rural Gloucestershire.

As if rubbing shoulders with the next King of England wasn't enough to give them a serious dose of the jitters, they also had to contend with a spotlight from the world's Press beaming right at them. Their interview with Prince Charles was, after all, only one of the few times the Prince had formally granted a TV interview.

'He turned out to be a very funny and charming man,' enthused Ant, not remotely fazed by the fact that he and Dec were aged 25 while the Prince was 52.

Dec revealed that the Prince had also asked the boys to become ambassadors for the Prince's Trust. 'We were flattered that he asked us,' he admitted.

It is understood that the Prince's two sons, William and Harry, were highly enthusiastic about Ant and Dec conducting the chat with their dad.

Tom Shebbeare, chief executive of the Trust, confirmed that when Ant and Dec met the Prince the conversation had flowed freely. 'I suppose Ant and Dec are rather a surprising choice [for the interview] but it came from a desire to reach those people who might not watch David Frost,' he told the *Mirror*. 'They got on like a house on fire. It was great to see how the Prince can identify with people of that age group and get on very well with them. Our target group might never have heard about the Prince's Trust but they might listen to Ant and Dec and realise then what the Trust could do for them.'

Dec was simply doing his job as a TV professional – but as far as his proud dad was concerned, his son's scoop with the Prince made for an electrifying day, full of excitement and celebrations. Dec's royal exclusive sent shockwaves through the Donnelly family household. Alphonsus was brimming with pride: 'I would never have dreamt my son would be hob-nobbing with royalty. I spoke to Declan before the interview and he said they were both excited but very nervous. They have interviewed some pretty famous people before but never a prince. Afterwards, they said he was a very nice bloke and they had got on like a house on fire. Prince Charles was keen to show them round his gardens and they all seemed quite relaxed. I don't think we would have ever imagined when he was a young lad that he would be interviewing members of the royal family. We are so proud. Both our Dec and Ant have come a long way.'

The interview, conducted in Highgrove's lavish gardens, was screened on Sunday 8 July 2001 on ITV as part of *The Party in the Park* in London. There was also a 'taster' snippet of the interview screened on Ant and Dec's Saturday ITV show *SM:tv Live*.

'He turned out to be a very funny and charming man.'

ANT & DEC 'One is a Great Admirer of Phil Collins...'

During the interview, Phil Collins, the legendary singer-songwriter, drummer and former Genesis frontman, emerged as one of Prince Charles's all-time favourite artists. It was Phil who in the early 1980s became one of the Prince's Trust's first, most high-profile and successful celebrity trustees, a VIP role which Phil felt honoured to play for over 15 years. Throughout the 80s and 90s, he worked tirelessly to drum up support from other famous artists for the many fundraising events that were staged to support the Trust. Thanks to his persuasive manner and his bulging contacts book, a huge array of international music stars turned out for the Prince's Trust – Eric Clapton, the three former Beatles George, Paul and Ringo, Sting, the Bee Gees, George Michael and Tina Turner, to name but a few. Proceeds from Phil's Genesis concerts and his 1988 movie premiere of *Buster*, co-starring Julie Walters, also went to the Trust, and Phil helped the prince and his advisers raise the profile of the Trust, especially among the young people it was set up to help.

These youngsters, of course, made up the very same audience that Ant and Dec were now reaching with their Highgrove interview. And as their conversation with HRH became more relaxed and informal, it also touched on the subject of the Prince's personal taste in music. Prince Charles revealed that, while he enjoys live music, he sometimes finds it deafening. 'There is nothing to beat live music, whether it's classical, or pop, or anything, I think,' said the Prince, adding that he was also a fan of Welsh band Catatonia and singer Tom Jones – jazz and classical music too. 'Sometimes I stagger out unable to hear anything,' he joked. 'Phil Collins [once] gave me a pair of earplugs!'

Prince Charles told Ant and Dec, 'I'm not an expert by any means on the latest scene because I can't keep up with all the changes.'

Prince Charles described Tom Jones as an 'astonishing phenomenon' and confided that he was 'keen' on Diana Ross.

Dec boldly asked the Prince, 'What do you enjoy relaxing and listening to in your personal time?' HRH told Dec, 'I do enjoy classical music but I'm keen on jazz, and also a great admirer of Phil Collins, Jools Holland and Elton John. And I did used to rather love the Dire Straits. Tremendous – a great band.'

When Ant and Dec pointed out that Dire Straits were fellow Geordies, the Prince joked, 'They're all over the shop!'

Tyneside no doubt enjoyed that quip ...

The seven minutes of the interview that were broadcast were actually the best bits from about an hour that the three of them spent chatting in the gardens. The conversation also took in, of course, the work that the Prince carries out with the Trust which he explained had started on a small scale in 1976. Today, it has helped 400,000 young people.

'We have different programmes to help address specific challenges and problems,' the Prince of Wales told Ant and Dec. 'It's so heartening to see people transformed. I just feel it's an investment in the future.'

Towards the end of their time with the Prince, Ant and Dec asked HRH if his sons, Princes William and Harry, would be getting involved in the Prince's Trust. Prince Charles reckoned

it was 'up to them really', adding, 'but you never know.'

HRH, Ant and Dec shared a final moment or two chatting away some more in the garden. Then it was time to go. It had been a truly amazing day.

Ant and Dec had hugely enjoyed their time with Prince Charles. For them, the royal journalistic scoop he had granted them marked a day they would never forget.

The boys from Newcastle ended the day leaving his company in a star-struck daze, knowing that everyone back home, their family, their friends and colleagues, all greatly admired what they had achieved.

10

The Price of Fame

It was a blissfully quiet, sunny morning as Ant strolled sleepily into his kitchen to pop the kettle on for a nice refreshing cup of tea.

He rubbed his eyes and stared out of the kitchen window to see a light summer's breeze gently sweeping across the garden. The birds in the trees were chirping and cheeping, daffodils bowed their heads and Ant's freshly laundered clothes, just out of the machine, danced in the wind, as they dried on the washing line.

Suddenly, as if from nowhere, a grasping hand reached up to commit a dastardly deed ... it grabbed a pair of Ant's knickers from the line! The thieving hand hurriedly tugged at the celebrity smalls as the clothes pegs went flying. And then she was gone – a teenage girl sprinting off down the road, Ant's undies in her hand.

Ant – now rubbing his eyes even harder – was left to reflect on the price of fame. And the loss of his pants.

Dec loves that story. And he enjoys telling a similar tale of his own. It relates to the day he was standing in a urinal, answering the call of Nature, when a man wandered up to him.

'Oh, it's you,' said the man. He was on his mobile phone at the time – and when he recognised Dec he tried to hand the phone over to him. 'Here,' he said, 'will you speak to my daughter?'

Dec didn't have a hand free.

Unlike more 'precious' celebrities we could mention, Ant and Dec have always made a point of signing autographs whenever asked (assuming their hands are free). They never refuse to sign one.

'It only takes a minute to say "How y'doing pal?" and sign their book. Then they skip away, quite happy,' says Ant. 'It's hardly a pain in the arse.'

'It only takes a minute to say "How y'doing pal?"'

Posters of Ant and Dec decorate thousands of girls' bedroom walls, and when love-struck girls sent in their undies by post, Ant says he used to blush at first. But then he'd write back saying that, with regret, they were the wrong size and colour.

One of the weirdest letters Dec ever received from a fan was the one sent him by a woman who wanted to tie him up with her bras and hold him hostage. Female fans' obsessions with Ant and Dec sometimes became a little too over-enthusiastic for the boys' taste – like when the lads' touring van was damaged by girls writing their names and addresses on the side in indelible ink.

One Dec fan changed her name by deed poll to Declan Donnelly. Some Geordie families regularly christen their children after their two TV idols, while Newcastle pet owners have even been known to name their dogs Ant and Dec.

'We once stopped at a service station on the way to a gig,' recalls Ant. 'A bloke who was carrying a baby came up to us and said, "It's a shame my wife isn't here. She's just had another little boy, and called him Declan." There he was, talking away, in spite of the fact that his wife had just named his new son after another man – after one of us, in fact.'

irl fans' enthusiasm also sometimes spilt on to the football terraces – as the lads once discovered when they turned out for a charity football match back home. A star-studded line-up arrived at Gateshead's International Stadium to take part in the event, which aimed to raise £25,000 for the Northeast centres of Marie Curie Cancer Care and the NSPCC.

The crowds applauded when the celebrities ran out on to the pitch. Ralf Little from TV's *The Royle Family* was there, so too Michael Greco from *EastEnders*, Peter Beardsley, John Fashanu, John Beresford and Frank McAvennie. Respectful applause and the odd cheer greeted those celebrities when they appeared. But when Ant and Dec took their place on the field the ground echoed to the raunchy chants of 'Sexy!' and 'Get your kit off!' – not slogans chanted by football crowds under normal circumstances.

After the game, the lads happily signed autographs for the fans – but that's as far as they went.

Nowadays, when Ant and Dec are working in London, they regularly feel homesick for the Northeast. And when they go home, they like nothing more than to head out on the town with their old mates. Touring the city's bars and clubs is far more enjoyable, they say, than mingling with celebrities at star-studded bashes, which are often little more than a media feeding frenzy anyway.

> '*I can't understand it when people forget where they came from,' says Dec with a frown. 'I never want to lose my accent and I don't want to forget all my mates. If you don't buy a round and you're making loads of money then you're a tight git. But if you get all the rounds in you're a flash git. You have to be careful to take your turn like everyone else.'*

Their experience at coping with fame was tested when Ant and Dec put in an appearance at the National TV Awards 2001. It brought home to them the fact that they had found fame in a major way – partly because they spent the evening of the awards ceremony mixing with the industry's most famous and successful people – *their peers*. The paparazzi had a field day and newspapers and magazines carried images of Ant and Dec at the bash for days, weeks, even months after the event.

ANT & DEC The Price of Fame

What makes the National TV Awards special is not the fact that nearly nine and a half million viewers tune in at home to watch the event. It is more the fact that it's those viewers themselves who cast the votes that decide the winners – unlike so many other showbusiness awards.

The 2001 event, held at London's Royal Albert Hall on Tuesday 23 October, and screened nationwide on ITV, found Ant and Dec up against Graham Norton and Michael Barrymore for the title of Most Popular Entertainment Presenter.

Before the National TV Awards ceremony got under way Ant and Dec had arrived with their girlfriends, Lisa Armstrong and Clare Buckfield, and had mingled with fellow celebrity guests. The lads looked elegant and dapper, wearing smart Mark Powell suits – Ant choosing a natty charcoal grey number with matching tie, while Dec looked sleek and chic wearing all black with a contrasting white tie.

Judging by the photos of the event, most of the guests were female! And the boys enjoyed rubbing shoulders with the cream of Britain's female celebrities, including *Grimleys* actress Amanda Holden, who won Most Popular Actress, singer Charlotte Church, *Countdown* hostess Carol Vorderman, sports presenter Kirsty Gallacher, and Patsy Kensit, ex-wife of Oasis star Liam Gallagher.

The soaps were well represented on the night, too. *EastEnders* cast members there included Lucy Benjamin, Tamzin Outhwaite and Jessie Wallace. From *Emmerdale* came Elspeth Brodie, Ruth Abram, Dee Whitehead and Anna Brecon, and the *Coronation Street* team comprised newly-wed Tracy Shaw, Jennifer James, Nikki Sanderson, Tina O'Brien, Clare McGlinn and Sally Lindsay.

Then came the moment of truth, as the nominations were read out. The atmosphere was electric – and then, suddenly, Ant and Dec found themselves walking up on stage. Boy band Blue stepped forward to present the Geordie duo with the Most Popular Entertainment Presenter award.

In the introductory speech, read out to introduce the lads, they had been described as 'giants' of the industry already. But Ant told the audience, 'I don't know why you called us giants of presenting, we're only five-foot-six! It's fantastic. I never thought we'd get it.'

And Dec, clutching their award, chipped in, 'I had a bet going that Graham Norton would win. I'm out of pocket now.'

The audience roared with laughter at the joke, as Dec added, 'I'm so happy. I'm going to get very drunk tonight...'

Looking back, Ant says, 'I don't know if you saw it but we were shocked. I really couldn't believe it. I was shaking and felt sick as we went up to collect our award. We felt privileged even to be nominated alongside such names as Michael Barrymore and Chris Tarrant. To win was beyond our wildest dreams. We came off stage to see Chris Tarrant applauding and giving us the thumbs up.'

Interviewed later, Tarrant generously endorsed his 'thumbs up' when asked about the lads: 'Ant and Dec are the best thing that has happened to kids' television – actually, *television* – for a very long time.'

After receiving their award, Dec added, 'We were really chuffed to be nominated because we hadn't even been to the awards before. We didn't prepare a speech and consequently looked like gibbering fools when we got up there.'

When all the nervous excitement had died down the fun started. Ant and Hear'Say's Myleene Klass let their hair down at the after-show party by inhaling helium from the balloons and launching into a high squeal version of the band's *Pure and Simple*, sounding like a cross between the Smurfs and Mickey Mouse.

The party was held at London's classy Royal College of Art, and was attended by hundreds of photographers and reporters. This ensured that the stars' every move was chronicled on screen and in print as they partied on into the small hours. It was a fairytale night that neither Ant nor Dec will forget.

On the question of Ant and Dec's identity, some newspaper pundits like to crack the old joke about how some people still don't know which one of the presenters is Ant and which is Dec. But Dec (he's the shorter one) has an answer ready. 'We have this cunning plan,' he explains obligingly. 'Whenever we're on telly or in photos, we always stand so that, left to right, it's always Ant...and...Dec.'

(One national newspaper which ran a photo of Ant and Dec on its front page mistakenly planned the layout with the picture reversed ... until an eagle-eyed executive who knew about Ant and Dec's 'left-to-right' trick spotted the error and alerted the production team in the nick of time!)

On a more serious and less frivolous note, there's another side to Ant and Dec's fame that rarely hits the headlines, but which is as important to them as the frothy glitz and glamour of the showbusiness world. The children's charity the NSPCC recently conducted a poll to find out who young people would choose to speak on their behalf on issues like bullying, child abuse and education. When the votes were in and counted, Ant and Dec emerged clear favourites, at the top of the list with more than 40 per cent of the vote. (Less popular names beaten by Ant and Dec included Prince William, Robbie Williams and Britney Spears.)

'The poll was conducted as part of our research into the need for a "children's commissioner" in England,' an NSPCC official explains. 'Such a commissioner would be a champion, a watchdog, independent of government, who would represent children's views and concerns. From the feedback we received, young people clearly felt that Ant and Dec could communicate well with children and young people, but equally with adults. This is a unique quality, as many people have credibility with one audience or the other, but not both.

'Ant and Dec are popular. They don't beat around the bush and they seem to be people who speak out rather than toe the line on important issues. Ant and Dec have helped the NSPCC with a number of projects in the past and we much appreciate their willingness to lend a hand. We are very grateful to them.'

The National Society for the Prevention of Cruelty to Children is a hugely respected charity and a noble cause that Ant and Dec, among other celebrities, are proud to support. But news of their victory in this recent young people's poll surprised even them. It made them take stock of their fame – and reflect on some of the unusual places it can sometimes lead them to.

But one of their biggest fans was even more surprised and delighted than they were by the accolade. The fan's name? Well, it's Mrs McPartlin, better known as Ant's lovely mam, Christine. At the family home back in Newcastle, when Christine found out about the poll, and the respect that her young son had come to command from children and young people right across the country, she was quite overcome with emotion at what a great honour it was.

She hugged her son...and burst into tears.

Top 10 Loves, Hates and Fears

Ant and Dec own up to having loads of pet hates, but equally there are people and places they love, too. And although they appear confident, they have fears just like the rest of us. Here's a round-up of the Top 10 things that turn them on ... and off.

ANT

1   LOVES: Ant's favourite TV show is *The Simpsons*.

2   HATES: And he hates the soaps.

3   FEARS: Ant is terrified of spiders. 'Spiders make me feel faint,' he admits.

4   LOVES: Ant has a 'thing' about footwear – he's the Imelda Marcos of ITV! 'I like fancy, weird moccasins and smart shoes,' he once told fans.

5   LOVES: Ant's all-time favourite yummy ice cream flavour is strawberry. Mmm, fruity!

DEC

1 LOVES: Looking elegant. When he was 14, Dec had a colourful collection of rather natty waistcoats.

2 FEARS: Dec's biggest phobia is of pigeons. Whenever one flies near him he ducks. He admits he's terrified of them, and says he imagines their beaks pecking at his eyes.

3 HATES: Dec hates nothing more than Alfred Hitchcock's famous movie thriller *The Birds* – his idea of hell!

4 LOVES: One of Dec's favourite books is Roald Dahl's *Charlie and the Chocolate Factory*.

5 LOVES: All the television comedy he grew up on – like *Morecambe and Wise*, the *Two Ronnies*, *Terry and June*, *Auf Wiedersehen Pet* and *Russ Abbot's Madhouse*. He's also a big Kenny Everett fan.

Pop Goes the Idol

Ant and Dec weren't the first guys to have suffered heartache at the hands of the lovely Ulrika Jonsson. Whether they'll be the last, only time will tell. Ulrika's BBC show *Dog Eat Dog* had seen off Ant and Dec's *Slap Bang* series – which was a disappointment to the lads' fans and, no doubt, to the presenters themselves.

But pretty soon, in their customary style, the Geordie boys were to bounce right back into the ratings and double their viewing figures to eight million almost overnight.

The return of their high profile was thanks to a gripping new entertainment show which captured not only the nation's attention but also many of the tabloids' front pages as well.

The series was to become a talking point in millions of homes around the country every Saturday night. Two simple words were to spark debate up and down the country between disagreeing relatives, disputes between youngsters and their parents.

Pop Idol.

The format couldn't have been simpler. Public auditions were to be held in a hunt to find a new British solo singer, a superstar worthy of the label 'pop idol'.

But the public reaction to the show was less easy to grasp. A staggering 10,000 people applied for an audition. The producers had stumbled on a monster hit and, even before the show got on the air in October 2001, it had clearly fired up the public's imagination.

Eight million viewers started tuning into the show each week during the early rounds, and audience figures rose higher still as the competition for the *Pop Idol* crown narrowed.

The 10,000 wannabe contestants were auditioned in London, Glasgow and Manchester and it was Ant and Dec's job to roam among the youngsters at auditions, chatting to them and generally making them feel at ease – while gleaning from them some of their individual and often fascinating stories.

Ant and Dec also witnessed some amazing extra talents the contestants displayed in the corridors while awaiting their auditions. Apart from playing a variety of instruments, they showed off their skills at breakdancing, handstands, rolling their tongues … and one girl proudly showed off how she could slot five 50p coins into her tummy button.

Of course there were a few 'singers' who really couldn't sing at all, and who immediately failed to make the grade. But the quality and range of those competing proved a huge surprise to the audience at home. The standard of many contestants was amazingly high – a fact acknowledged by some established stars like Dannii Minogue. Dannii, who appeared on *cd:uk* during the run of *Pop Idol*, paid tribute to the amateur contestants. She reckoned quite a few 'professional' singers who had already become established would struggle to pass *Pop Idol* auditions, because they had already become used to the luxury of having dancers and glitzy sets to support them.

As for the contestants' determination to succeed, that provided some unexpected moments of entertainment too. Some hopefuls went to any lengths to get through – usually they failed.

*T*he age restrictions for *Pop Idol* were strict, but one female contestant was so desperate to be chosen as a finalist that she lied about her age to the judges, claiming she was 21. She blagged her way in front of the panel, who immediately raised an eyebrow at her rather 'mature' appearance. They admired her determination – but, sadly, less so her talent – and after her efforts it emerged that she was, in fact, a 32-year-old mother of six!

Ant and Dec attended a few of the early auditions themselves, and found the experience highly entertaining. 'We only sat in on a few, just to see the judging process, and then we were at the back and out of view,' says Ant. 'But there were times I was really killing myself. I wouldn't have laughed in front of them, because that could destroy someone's confidence. But one time we were laughing so much we were told to get out.'

Dec adds, 'You really try not to laugh. Honest to God, you do. We've both been in auditions over the years and it's a really intimidating environment. But you look at some people and think, "Why have you come?"'

'Some of them were a bit deluded. Our job was just to chat to hopefuls. And we had it all – the tears, people getting angry, people wanting to go back in and do it again, or have an argument with the judges. If you wrote any of what happened, people would say it was too far-fetched.'

The contestants may have reduced Ant and Dec to hysterics on occasions, but there were also times when the duo were humbled by the youngsters they met. In fact, at one point, Ant and Dec were left speechless.

'They shared their dreams and innermost feelings with us and you couldn't help but feel for them when they had to go home,' says Dec. 'You felt how much they wanted it. We had been through it ourselves when we were going for acting parts, and it's very hard not to take the rejection personally. That night, we went down the pub and sat in silence, probably for the first time ever, thinking about how those who didn't make it must have been feeling.'

In contrast the pair found it thrilling to meet so many larger-than-life personalities during the auditions. 'Every day there would be characters,' Dec explains. 'If you put some of them in a script, people wouldn't believe it. There was the 48 year-old Indian man who couldn't speak English. He didn't want to sing, he just wanted to recite some Hindu poetry.'

Ant adds, 'There were singing Elvises in full costume, one with a wooden leg. There was one girl wearing a lacy top and we jokingly said to her, "Are you wearing your mam's net curtains?" And she said, "Yeah, I am!" She had these white trousers but no top to go with them so had cut down her mam's net curtains.'

Dec butts in, 'She said, "If I don't get through the audition, I've got to sew them back into a pair of curtains."'

She didn't get through.

During the early rounds, some of the series' great characters fell by the wayside, like Darius Danesh (later reinstated), who became infamous for his big head in the preceding series, *Popstars*.

As the rounds sifted the rough from the smooth, the reappearing Darius got smoother – by shaving off his goatee beard and moustache to present the judges with a new clean-cut image. But his cosmetic changes failed to impress the viewers at home sufficiently.

At one point, cheeky Ant and Dec decided to take the mickey out of Darius for a joke. Dec donned a wig and false goatee beard to perform a hilarious impression of Darius behind his back. Darius, who had been branded 'corny' by judge Simon Cowell, became infamous for his flowery expressions and Dec quickly got in on the act. Spoofing Darius's patter, Dec gushed, 'There are a lot of shattered dreams and broken hearts out there. A week in *Pop Idol* is just a drop in time.'

Astonishingly, the eventual winner of *Pop Idol* turned out to be the very last contestant of the original 10,000 to apply to take part. William Young, 23, from Hungerford in Berkshire, is a well-spoken, middle-class chap with a cheesy smile. A company director's son, Will was a pupil at Wellington public school and he graduated in politics from Exeter University – not exactly your stereotypical pop idol.

The final, broadcast live on ITV on 9 February 2002, did more than capture the nation's imagination – it created British TV history by becoming the country's most successful ever television talent show, culminating in Britain's biggest ever TV vote.

On the night, Will was up against rival finalist and bookies' favourite Gareth Gates, 17, a postman's son from Bradford, West Yorkshire. Gareth had already won millions of fans with his singing voice. A reported 15 million viewers tuned in and, by the end of the competition, a staggering 8.7 million votes had been cast for the two finalists. That's more votes than were cast for the Conservative Party during the previous year's General Election (8.4 million).

While the show gripped the general public at home, in the TV studio the two contestants' families mingled in the audience with established stars. Celebrities who came to pay their respects and watch the show live included singers Annie Lennox and Charlotte Church, and actors Tony Robinson and Tamzin Outhwaite. Gareth also received a 'good luck' e-mail from Westlife, his own pop idols.

Later it emerged that Will and Gareth each had a celebrity following of their own on the night. Stars supporting Will included Robbie Williams, Victoria Beckham and Michelle Collins, while Gareth's fans were Richard and Judy, Denise Van Outen and former Steps singer Faye Tozer. S Club 7 also reportedly sent Will a message saying, 'Hope to see you in the charts and we'll help you celebrate being number one.'

Will and Gareth went head-to-head in the live final, which was divided into sections and spread across the ITV evening schedule. Both boys sang their hearts out with *Evergreen* and *Anything is Possible*, the two songs to be featured on a record the winner would release. As the end of the show neared, nerves were jangling when Ant and Dec gave viewers at home a voting update.

As the last segment of the final kicked off, Will admitted, 'I could feel my legs turning to jelly!'

At the climax of the show, Ant and Dec stepped forward alongside the two finalists to announce the viewers' verdict. Dec told Will and Gareth, 'As you both know, guys, there can only be *one* pop idol. Best of luck to the pair of you.'

Tension reached fever pitch as it then fell to Ant to deliver the line the nation was waiting to hear: 'The winner of Pop Idol 2002 is ... Will.'

'I could feel my legs turning to jelly!'

Will gasped – in fact, he nearly fainted. The audience in the studio, and in homes around the country, went berserk. Afterwards, Ant told him, 'Your face! I thought you were going to keel over!'

As Will later explained, 'When I realised it was me who'd won it took probably a second to sink in, but it seemed like minutes. Ant and Dec grabbed me to say congratulations and that was probably a good thing because, if they hadn't, I'd have slid to the floor in shock.'

On the night the phone lines almost went into meltdown. It emerged that 4.6 million votes had been cast for Will, compared to 4.1 million for Gareth. British Telecom, who laid on 28,000 lines, were reported to have made £11million from the phone vote; the public rang in at a mind-boggling rate of 50,000 calls a second. The flood of calls even disrupted emergency services across the country as lines to ambulance stations were blocked.

The total number of phone votes cast during the entire series was an estimated 32 million. For some time after the final was screened, a row rumbled on in the tabloids about how many people were unable to vote because the lines were jammed. It was reported that a staggering 80 million call attempts were made *within two hours* as viewers clamoured to register their preference. That's equivalent to three-quarters of all the calls made in Britain in an average 24 hours. Pretty staggering statistics.

None of this prevented the winner Will, instantly dubbed 'William The Conquerer' by the newspapers, from emerging victorious and something of a national hero. He landed a big-money contract with 19 Management, the team who launched the Spice Girls and S Club 7, and a recording deal. In fact, both Will and Gareth were snapped up by the label BMG, for whom record producer and *Pop Idol* judge Simon Cowell is a consultant. According to the newspapers, both singers were immediately set on the road to become multi-millionaires through music industry contracts, endorsements and merchandising deals.

Inevitably, some fans questioned whether Ant and Dec might themselves be tempted to relaunch their music careers after being so closely involved with *Pop Idol*. Pete Waterman offered them the chance to return to the recording studio, where they had launched their pop star careers after *Byker Grove*. But the

boys tactfully and firmly declined. Dec insists, 'We got away with it for three years, but there's not much demand for our return. Pete Waterman has asked us but I don't think we'll be stepping back into our music shoes.'

wo things became clear as *Pop Idol* drew to a close. First, what a wealth of untapped talent lay hidden out there; the quality of the top contestants certainly surprised the judges. And second, everyone was surprised – both on the show and at home – by how desperately the youngsters taking part craved fame. Fame was the drug; fame was their goal and they were going after it.

They spoke to Ant and Dec during auditions about how badly they craved fame, and the boys, having served their time as pop idols themselves, knew from personal experience that the winner of the series would have a real struggle on their hands – coping with fame.

Ant and Dec had learned their own 'fame' lessons the hard way. Their profile hadn't stopped rising since their early success as teenagers on *Byker Grove*, and they both knew that fame brought with it a string of pressures that were never easy to cope with.

Sure, it's great for the ego and self-confidence, pretty flattering that record company executives and television producers all want a part of you. But the flip-side of the coin is that fame means *everyone* wants a part of you.

That means that when fame hits you, you become public property to some degree. The media feeding frenzy begins, and newspaper photographers follow you everywhere. All the fans are keen to grab a chunk of you.

Not everyone can handle those unwelcome pressures and strains, as Ant and Dec both know full well ...

JOKES AND JAPES

Ant and Dec love a laugh. Larking about in the studio comes naturally to them because they believe that having fun is the name of the game. Here are ten of the Tyneside Twosome's funniest jokes and japes.

1   IT'S GOTTA RHYME:

Kids phoning in to guess the right answer to Wonkey Donkey drove Dec crazy each week when they forgot the golden rule: It's Gotta Rhyme! (e.g. Mersey Jersey, Snotty Scottie, Tuna Crooner, Scouse Mouse, Asleep Sheep, Weaver Retriever, etc.) When kids' answers *didn't* rhyme Dec blew a fuse, often shouting rudely at contestants. His best insults included:

- 'Noel Mule? And that rhymes in your part of the world, does it?'

- 'Sorry, luv, this is *SM:tv Live*. I think you've got the wrong number. We're playing Wonkey Donkey. Do you understand the game? It doesn't sound like it. Now go away!'

- 'You shouldn't have bothered ringing in really, should you?'

- 'Don't be stupid, will you man? That doesn't rhyme!'

2   GUN GAG BACKFIRES:

Ant and Dec love using daft props, and once, for a joke, they used a plastic toy pistol on their show *Slap Bang*. Dec was chatting to *Coronation Street* star Bill Roach (who plays Ken Barlow in the soap) and Ant kept interrupting. Finally, Bill and Ant stormed off – and Dec drew a plastic gun and shot at them. ITV insisted, 'The whole sketch was a broad farce, with over-the-top gusto in the best tradition of knockabout comedy. The gun in the scene was a plastic toy pistol and clearly not real.' But the gun gag backfired – the Broadcasting Standards Commission upheld a viewer's complaint and ruled against the show.

3   ATOMIC SMITTEN:

Ant, Dec and Cat did a take-off of Atomic Kitten called 'Atomic Smitten'. The boys played Liz and Natasha from the band. Liz (Ant) said her favourite perfume was Essence of Chippy, Natasha (Dec) sported a love bite called 'Midnight Bus Stop'. Cat played Jenny.

4 DIGESTIVE SUGGESTIVE:

Dec says, 'Once we asked viewers to send their embarrassing dad stories to us to read on the show [*SM:tv*]. But before we went on air Ant said, "I've got a story to read but I'm not going to tell you it until we're live." It was about this dad who'd fart in the family biscuit tin, close the lid quickly, then offer the tin round to friends! We all got hysterics – I couldn't stop! I just kept imagining this bloke with his bum over the tin!'

5 IGNOR-ANT!:

On *SM:tv* one of the best jokes was on Ant! He recalls, 'Once we did a live sketch, but I thought it was just a rehearsal. I wandered on set going "What camera am I supposed to be looking at?" and mumbling my lines. Slowly I realised what was going on, but I had to carry on as if nothing had happened and it was all part of the sketch! I was so embarrassed.'

6 LYING MAIDEN:

Dec recalls one of his most daring japes. He says, 'When I was a nipster my fave band was Iron Maiden. Unfortunately, I'd told my mates that the lead singer was my brother and that he'd get us into the gig – so when they did a gig nearby, I had to think fast. With the help of an old shoebox, cut out to look like a stage, some Star Wars figures (the band) and a ghetto blaster hidden by a tree, I created my own 'mini-gig' and placed it at the end of a field. Then I set up a tent about 500 metres away and pretended I'd broken my leg. When my mates arrived they felt so sorry for me that they watched the 'gig' from the tent and actually believed it was Iron Maiden! (Well, until I had to turn the tape over!)'

7 STAR SPOT:

In his Agony Uncle column in *cd:uk* magazine, Dec reveals how Ant deals with facial spots in the morning. Answering a letter from a young reader who had just started shaving, Dec writes, 'Ant is always moaning about having to shave and moisturise daily. His dashing looks are often spoilt by scraps of Andrex which cover the places where he's shaved his plooks too. Ouch!'

Pop Idol: Bits and Pieces

The nasty, hyper-critical judges on *Pop Idol* were 'as harsh as sandpaper underpants', as Ant delicately put it. But that didn't stop them providing compulsive viewing as they hooked the nation's viewers in their millions. Amid all the frenzy and excitement you may have missed some of the fun, behind-the-scenes details from the show. So here's a round-up of some extra juicy bits to enjoy.

1   Nicki Chapman looked the sincerest and friendliest of the judges. In Ant and Dec's *cd:uk* magazine she even offered contestants four useful tips in the run-up to the programme. These rules apply to hopefuls everywhere, so if you're planning on being a pop star, remember:

• BE CONFIDENT: 'It's nerve-wracking, but if you can't be confident at an audition, what happens when you play Wembley?'

• BE BRAVE: 'Think of what the judges want. If you're going to a *Pop Idol* audition, don't arrive looking like Marilyn Manson and moaning about pop!'

• LOOK GOOD: 'Don't overdress, but make an effort. You don't want to look like you're just there on the off chance.'

• BE TALENTED: 'Be honest with yourself – if you can't sing, it just ain't gonna happen!'

2   Judge Simon Cowell, now the boss of RCA Records, owns up to a fatal error of judgement in his early career – he once gave the thumbs down to Take That. 'I turned them down with the words, "I think they might be huge but they should lose the fat one," and with every Number-one hit they had I felt physically ill!'

3   Simon's skill at picking winners throughout his career has made him a multi-millionaire. He lives in London's expensive Holland Park, drives an Aston Martin and races go-karts in his spare time.

4   But Simon wasn't always rich and infamous. He started work in the music business as a humble post boy at EMI when he was just 17.

5 Judge Pete Waterman was nicknamed Pete 'Slaughterman' by TV colleagues after he became infamous for his ultra-rude put-downs on the show.

6 Pete's hobby is steam trains – he owns nine of them.

7 Finalist Gareth Gates revealed himself as a recovering stammerer when he took 20 seconds to pronounce his own name. He then amazed the judges by launching into his first-round audition with a flawless performance of his song, *Flying Without Wings*. His mum Wendy burst into tears when she heard him speak without stammering.

8 In October 2001, when Ant and Dec were guests on Frank Skinner's ITV chat show, they dressed up in drag to mimic *Pop Idol*'s YMCA girl contestant. She promptly jumped up on stage herself and joined in.

'Nasty' Simon Cowell mastered the art of the cruel 'put-down' and regularly left *Pop Idol* contestants quaking in their boots or bursting into tears. Here's my all-time favourite Top 10 of his most cutting and caustic comments.

☹ 'Distinctly average, I'm afraid.'

☹ 'What if I told you you couldn't sing?'

☹ 'Honestly, that was terrible. Obviously you've got a day job!'

☹ 'It's pointless going on. You're not cut out to be a pop star at all.'

☹ 'You sound like Mickey Mouse on helium.'

☹ 'Are you serious? You can't sing. You can't dance.'

☹ 'That was awful. You do all boy bands a disservice.'

☹ 'I'm sort of speechless. I don't know what to say, it was just weird. I'm actually surprised you got this far. I don't think you should be here. Sorry!'

☹ 'I'm afraid to say that really hurt my ears!'

☹ 'Mark yourself out of 10 on that.' (Contestant gives himself seven. Simon disagrees.) 'Two.'

Where to Next, Eh?

'We're looking at other things. The next step in our career is going to be a big one,' Dec prophetically told the *Newcastle Evening Chronicle* back in November 2000. 'We're going to concentrate on it and make sure it's the right thing to do. We're developing projects – a game show, a sitcom and a comedy-drama.'

Ant was equally excited about what the future might hold. 'We'd like to make a return to acting and we're working on an idea for a comedy-drama,' he confided. 'We'd also like to do a sitcom but they are so hard to get right.'

Ant and Dec were also reported to have long been in secret talks with ITV network boss David Liddiment about their plans to switch to mainstream, 'grown-up' TV.

After the Geordie duo's departure from *SM:tv Live* in December 2001, Cat Deeley took over as the main anchor on the show. According to reports in the media, BBC bosses offered Cat a £1million contract and her own show in an effort to turn her head away from ITV and sign her up as a prime-time BBC star. Weeks after Ant and Dec quit *SM:tv*, Cat announced she was leaving the show herself after being bombarded with offers to front other programmes, including a holiday series, another entertainment format, and a starring role in a major new drama.

Ant and Dec couldn't have been more pleased for their chum. The boys had already secured their own big-money deal with ITV, reportedly for more than £2million, but despite all the material benefits contracts like that deliver, the lads from Newcastle held true to their working-class roots. They wanted to work. 'We wanted a bit of security. We want to have a mortgage, a home and enough money to feel secure for the rest of our lives. I still want to keep working,' Ant explains. 'The houses and stuff just represent a little bit of security to be going on with.'

Ant and Dec have also turned their eyes towards the British film industry, and there have been approaches from a number of independent production companies.

*H*aving made such an impressive early mark in their careers on the small screen, the Geordie duo felt encouraged to broaden their horizons. In October 2001, chatting to the *Sun*, Ant sounded almost surprised by his own success: 'Things are going amazingly well. We are being offered so much. In the past few months quite a few British-based film companies have approached us and said, "We'd love to work with you." It's our ambition to star in a great British comedy. I haven't quite got over the flattery of being asked. There are so many fantastic writers, producers and directors in Britain. We'd love to be part of that. We are going to jump at the chance. It's a dream come true.'

Some papers have reported that the pair have been 'inundated with film offers' but are hanging on for a decent script. Dec seems to have his feet firmly on the ground. 'We've got no idea about the film industry, so we're taking a bit of advice and waiting for the right one to come along. It would have to be a funny one though.'

On the TV front, Ant and Dec are planning a high-profile return to our small screens in 2002. As this book goes to print, the format of their comeback show is expected to be a live Saturday evening programme on ITV. The show will be fun-packed and is likely to follow a similar tone to the *SM:tv Live* they left behind – with the one major difference, of course: that the content of the new series will be aimed at a slightly older audience.

By pulling out of *SM:tv Live* when it was at the height of its success – and taking the decision apparently days after they had been honoured as Most Popular Entertainment Presenters – Ant and Dec sent a clear signal to the industry, and the public, that they were determined not to get stuck in a rut. They were ready to change their image once again.

On the other hand, larking about and having fun with members of the audience is what Ant and Dec know they're good at – and their producers know it too. Which is why they are unlikely to depart too radically from their tried-and-tested style. 'It'll be lots of fun. We'll muck about as much as we do on *SM:tv Live*. That's what we're good at,' says Ant.

Caught in an unusually frank and soul-baring frame of mind, Ant makes no secret of how emotional it is for him and Dec to be leaving children's TV. 'Yes. It's weird, and a bit of a wrench,' he admits. 'But we do have a clear vision of where we want to go. ITV are keen to keep us in a family audience position, such as a primetime Saturday evening slot.'

Dec chips in, 'It is a big step. We'll just have to suck it and see.'

And then there's *Pop Idol* – the second series. At the end of the final Dec let slip that plans were already under way to produce a follow-up series, provisionally titled *Pop Idol Two*. He told viewers, 'Next time it could be you up here. If you think you've got what it takes, stay tuned for the address.'

And later it emerged that *Pop Idol*'s producers and judges had already held talks with ITV bosses about auditions for a second series. Plans were being drawn up for another nationwide trawl for a second pop idol.

If the second series goes ahead, Ant and Dec have said they would be keen to act as hosts once again. 'I don't know what they [the producers] are planning yet, but if there is another one we'd love to get involved,' said Ant. Millions of fans hope they do.

There was even talk of the show being exported to America, with the prospect of some of its key cast members becoming international stars.

Another singing project also looming would see Ant and Dec having the spotlight on *themselves*. This time, they would take centre stage, not as pop heart-throbs PJ and Duncan, but as soccer-mad Ant and Dec.

The lads are reported to have been targeted by the Football Association, who want them to sing this year's official England World Cup anthem. A source at the FA was quoted as saying, 'Ant and Dec are the ones we want. They're massive Newcastle supporters and know a lot about football. And they're also the most popular people on TV. We're hoping to recreate the buzz David Baddiel and Frank Skinner's *Three Lions* had during Euro '96. That sold a million and we think that with Ant and Dec's appeal, they could beat that.'

riends of the Tyneside pair told the *Mirror* that Ant and Dec would be thrilled if it happened. 'They worship Newcastle,' confided a friend. 'When they were kids they wanted to play for the team. They were never good enough – but this would be the next best thing.'

2001 was Ant and Dec's best and busiest year yet. Apart from appearing in a string of TV series, in children's slots and during primetime for family audiences, they found time to record a Christmas TV commercial for Woolworths and voice-overs for McDonald's hamburger adverts – and when big names in the high street start snapping you up as a presenter, you know you've hit the mainstream market.

2002 will no doubt bring the two tornadoes from Tyneside further success, as they continue to storm the TV ratings and whip up a frenzy of excitement among their fans.

Somehow, Ant and Dec always manage to exude a happy-go-lucky, game-for-a-laugh approach to everything they touch. As their catchphrase suggests, they know where it's at. And we'll carry on tuning in because we so much enjoy sharing their company.

Especially as it seems, just like us, they're...*Loving Every Second!*

Alec Lom

Alec Lom has worked as a writer for the past 20 years, as a Fleet Street journalist, television script writer and author. The son of an actor, he specialised in showbusiness while working on newspapers like the *Daily Mirror* before joining BBC TV's entertainment department. A former writer and researcher on *This Is Your Life*, he has a number of celebrity books to his name, and recently ghosted the autobiographies of TV presenters Jim Davidson and Jeremy Beadle. Alec is married with two children and lives in London.

Credits

In gathering background research material for this book, I am indebted to and wish to thank the following publications, whose contributions I gratefully acknowledge:

The *Catholic Agency For Overseas Development* magazine, *cd:uk* magazine, the *Daily Mirror*, the *Daily Telegraph*, *Heat* magazine, *Hello* magazine, the *Mail on Sunday*, the *Newcastle Evening Chronicle*, the *Newcastle Journal*, the *Newcastle Sunday Sun*, *Now!* magazine, *OK!* magazine, the *Scottish Daily Record*, the *Sun*, the *Sunday Times*, *The Times*, *TV Choice* magazine.

The author gratefully acknowledges the following for the use of pictures in this book:
North News and Pictures, *Newcastle Journal*, Redferns Picture Library, Retna Pictures, Des Willie, Rex Features, Alpha, Craig Barritt/Retnauk, Ken McKay (Rex Features), Aquarius Library, Terry Williams (Rex Features), Big Pictures Library, PA, Roslyn Guant and Blaze.